"Reading through Dr Sendjaya's book,
away that he is an articulate leadership
The book is filled with academic rese
teaching, wide exposure within both church and corporate world
and rich personal experiences. With a sharp and observant perspective, Dr Sendjaya challenges the conventional understanding of
leadership and unveils the biblical truth of gospel-centered leadership. Whether for seminary training, educational institutions, or to
expand one's understanding of biblical leadership, Dr Sendjaya's
book is unquestionably a reliable source to explore. It's truly a book
worth reading. I highly recommend it!"

—**Rev Dr Joshua Ting,** *General Secretary, Chinese*
Coordination Centre of World Evangelism

"Dr Sendjaya has written an important and practical guide for
leaders to adopt and develop a gospel-centered approach to leadership. The book is valuable for new leaders as well as seasoned
leaders and useful to all contexts of leadership whether com-
mercial, academic, government, Church, etc. Leadership advice
in the Bible can improve and strengthen any leader and Dr
Sendjaya does an excellent job of supporting the principles and
practices with scriptural concepts and examples of leaders in the
Bible. This book would make a great base for group discussions
about leadership as well as one-on-one leadership coaching
sessions."

—**Bruce E. Winston, PhD,** *Professor of Business and*
Leadership, Regent University School of Business &
Leadership, Virginia, USA

"In a world where leaders struggle to stay true to (or even find) a
moral compass, and where spirituality is no longer merely a private
affair, this book offers a clear picture of leadership that is driven
by Christian values and spirituality. How can Christians and other
people of faith lead their organizations on the basis of time-tested
religious principles, whether they serve in business, politics, education or other fields? Sen Sendjaya's reputation as a leadership

researcher and his expertise as a leadership educator make this an excellent resource that will indeed redeem leadership from a 'secular, neutral' perspective to invigorate it again with a sense of meaning and value that is rooted in the gospel."

—**Jack Barentsen, PhD,** *Professor of Practical Theology and Pastoral Leadership, Evangelische Theologische Faculteit, Leuven, Belgium*

"Drawing upon Scripture, as well modern business theory and practice, Sen Sendjaya has provided us with a timely reminder that effective Christian leaders must firstly be faithful followers of the Lord Jesus Christ. Sendjaya places the gospel at the centre of leadership, focussing on the primary importance of character over other traits and skills for effective leadership. A practical, readable and Christ-centred book that I hope will help shape our thinking about Christian leadership in the coming years. Highly recommended!"

—**Rev Stuart Coulton,** *Principal, Sydney Missionary and Bible College, Australia*

"Sen Sendjaya's book, *Leadership Reformed,* is a timely reminder that authentic Christian leadership is always in emulation of Christ. Sen tackles the egoism inherent in much contemporary leadership by applying the theological concept of sin and pointing to the need for redemption through faith in Christ leading to humility and self-sacrifice. Christian leaders are not immune from sinful and destructive behaviour, and organisational structures and practices are often inadequate in providing the necessary accountability to protect leaders from their dark side. Leadership grounded in faith in Christ and his Word is the only effective antidote. This book should be read by Christian leaders and by those to whom they are accountable. It combines a wealth of theological, theoretical and anecdotal insights to reinforce the central call for Christ-centred servant leadership."

—**Dr Stephen Fogarty,** *President, Alphacrucis College, Australia*

"This book contains a fascinating blend of spiritual, social, psychological and organisational insights, creating a tremendously helpful contribution to the field of Christian leadership. Sen Sendjaya manages the hard-to-achieve task of making scholarly writing accessible to the non-academic practitioner, and his use of in-the-trenches examples and illustrations makes it really practical. Thoughtful discussions on important leadership topics invite a more considered reflection by a reader who doesn't simply want a quick leadership fix."

—**Gary Williams,** *National Director, Christian Ministry Advancement (CMA), Australia*

Leadership Reformed

This book presents the gospel as a sensemaking tool to critically examine five areas of personal leadership effectiveness, namely desire, identity, dignity, motive, and ambition.

Every tipping point in changing the world for the better always involves leadership. Yet history also illustrates that even formidable leaders are prone to derailment and failures. Contrary to the popular idea that leaders need to enhance their self-efficacy to be effective, the focus of self is misguided because the self is the epicenter of the leadership problem. The author posits that the preoccupation with the self (and consequently, unbelief in the gospel) is the fundamental reason why leaders are blinded by power and control, create their own performance treadmill, live for the approval of others, and have myopic ambitions for things of this world.

Drawing on biblical insights and scholarly research, the leadership principles outlined in the book and their street-level applications will equip both novice and seasoned leaders to begin and end well.

Sen Sendjaya (PhD) is Professor of Leadership at Swinburne Business School, Australia. A leading scholar on servant leadership, Sen has published in top-ranked management journals and delivered leadership development workshops internationally. Sen is the author of *Personal and Organizational Excellence through Servant Leadership*.

Leadership Reformed

Why Leaders Need the Gospel to Change the World

Sen Sendjaya

Routledge
Taylor & Francis Group

LONDON AND NEW YORK

First published 2020
by Routledge
2 Park Square, Milton Park, Abingdon, Oxon OX14 4RN

and by Routledge
52 Vanderbilt Avenue, New York, NY 10017

Routledge is an imprint of the Taylor & Francis Group, an informa business

© 2020 Sen Sendjaya

British Library Cataloguing-in-Publication Data
A catalogue record for this book is available from the British Library

Library of Congress Cataloging-in-Publication Data
Names: Sendjaya, Sen, author.
Title: Leadership reformed : why leaders need the gospel to change the
    world / Sen Sendjaya.
Description: Abingdon, Oxon ; New York, NY : Routledge, 2020. |
    Includes bibliographical references and index.
Identifiers: LCCN 2019043699 (print) | LCCN 2019043700 (ebook) |
    ISBN 9781138193338 (hbk) | ISBN 9780367857516 (pbk) | ISBN
    9781315638188 (ebk)
Subjects: LCSH: Leadership—Religious aspects—Christianity.
Classification: LCC BV4597.53.L43 S46 2020 (print) | LCC BV4597.53.
    L43 (ebook) | DDC 658.4/092—dc23
LC record available at https://lccn.loc.gov/2019043699
LC ebook record available at https://lccn.loc.gov/2019043700

ISBN: 978-1-138-19333-8 (hbk)
ISBN: 978-0-367-85751-6 (pbk)
ISBN: 978-1-315-63818-8 (ebk)

Typeset in Palatino
by Apex CoVantage, LLC

Contents

Figures

Tables

Acknowledgements

A book comes into completion trailing clouds of inspiration from others. Many individuals helped me make this book a reality, or maintain my sanity in the process of writing it. I'd like to highlight a few in ascending order, from the least to most wonderful.

I dedicate this book to three individuals in my past life who shall remain nameless. They epitomized bad leadership. But unbeknownst to them, God worked mysteriously and taught me invaluable leadership lessons. I just have to remind myself to reverse each one of them. Thanks to them, I can begin to sympathize with Joseph, who wrote many centuries ago, 'As for you, you meant evil against me, but God meant it for good' (Genesis 50:20).

Many executives and professionals in my leadership workshops and MBA classes have prodded me to think clearly about many aspects of leadership. They have inspired and challenged my views, affirmed and stretched my imaginations, prompting me to get out of the ivory tower of academia and engage with real-world issues. I do hope that the pages that follow contain some wisdom, however little or much, that are written not from level 46 of that tower but from the street level.

As can be deduced from the references I cite in this book, I am greatly indebted to theologians, primarily dead theologians, who through their writings led me to experience the life-giving truth of the gospel of Christ Jesus. They have been instrumental in helping me integrate my dual roles as a business school professor and local church pastor. This book would otherwise be impossible without them.

To my better half, Dr Lyfie Sugianto, and children, Tiffany and Calvin, thanks for sticking with me over the years as you patiently witness my struggle to lead and live in a manner worthy of the gospel.

Finally, all that is excellent or praiseworthy in this book reflects that which comes from the Author of Life. All that falls short is from yours truly.

CHAPTER 1
What business schools don't teach you about leadership

'For what does it profit a leader to change the world and lose his soul?'
(an adaptation from Jesus' famous saying
in the gospel of Matthew)

Leadership matters

Every tipping point in the long arc of history of thoughtfully engaged individuals changing the world for the better always involves effective leadership. Martin Luther chose not to stand idle witnessing the deviations from orthodoxy, and accidentally launched the Protestant Reformation movement in the 16th century. A century later, Martin Luther King Jr. rose up to the challenge of racial segregation, and took the civil rights movement to the next level with its effects reverberating throughout the country.

We may never know who they were if they swapped their places in history. Yet because they dared to dream things that were against the status quo and became what T.S. Eliot famously called 'dreamers of day' who acted out their dreams with open eyes, the world became a better place to live in.

An organization might have superior talents, robust strategy, proprietary technology, or vast resources, but the absence of effective leadership will sooner or later erode these competitive advantages. That is true for all sorts of organizations, from small tech start-ups and church plants to multinational corporations and empires, and anything in between.

No doubt leadership is vital. Yet leaders are not infallible and invincible. History shows us time and again that even the most formidable leaders are prone to derailment and failures. The reason is deceptively simple. They are unable to handle the temptations that come with their leadership positions. Initially they manage power, then power manages them. For those occupying leadership roles, the risk of assault from the temptations of power, pride, popularity, and pleasure, to name a few, is always imminent. Countless leaders have fallen victims to these idols of the heart.

As such, while the idea of changing the world is noble, many are losing themselves in the process. To put a spin on a well-known saying by Jesus Christ that inspired the title of this book, the most important question to ask for aspiring leaders is 'For what does it profit a leader to change the world and lose his soul?'

[Disclaimer: I deliberately did not alter the male pronoun to a gender-inclusive pronoun because the overwhelming majority of individuals who lost their soul in their efforts to change the world through their organizations are male.]

Derailed Christian leader: A case in point

You may have heard about the following names: Bernard Ebbers of WorldCom Inc., Richard Scrushy of HealthSouth Corp, and Kenneth Lay of Enron. What commonality do they have in common? They were top leaders of three American multinational corporations who publicly and repeatedly professed their Christian faith.

Let us zero in on Ken Lay. He was the son of a Baptist minister and a faithful member of First United Methodist Church in Houston, Texas. And he did walk the talk too, donating millions of dollars every year to nonprofit organizations. Armed with a PhD in Economics, Lay climbed the corporate ladder of Houston Natural Gas and became its CEO in 1984. He masterfully orchestrated a series of mergers and acquisitions with InterNorth and formed Enron Corporation in 1985 (Cruver, 2003).

Under his leadership Enron pursued an aggressive diversification strategy that led the operation of gas pipelines, electricity plants, pulp and paper plants, water plants, and broadband services across the globe. The company market cap rose exponentially between 1996 and 2000 in excess of $60 billion, making it the sixth largest company in the US by sales. Fortune magazine hailed the company as America's most innovative large company for six consecutive years until 2001 (Bryce, 2003; Fusaro & Miller, 2002).

Then everything came crashing down. On December 2, 2001 Enron declared bankruptcy, the largest of its kind in US history at the time. Lay was convicted of conspiring to cover up corporate embezzlement and market-manipulating accounting schemes, including multiple counts of securities and wire fraud. He was sentenced for 45 years in prison but had heart attack and died before the sentencing began in July 2006 (McLean & Elkind, 2003; Swartz, 2003)

The spectacular collapse of Enron contains many lessons on leadership too precious to be ignored by any student of leadership. There are issues of leadership integrity, accountability, governance, greed, dark personality, to name a few, that can fill dozens of books. In the post-Enron world, efforts to understand why some leaders seem to deteriorate not long after they are installed into the throne while others withstand the temptations of power are urgently required.

Of all the questions that circulate around the popular and academic press on this case, the most interesting question is the one that I have been pondering for many years. What turned an otherwise formidable Christian leader with a strong faith upbringing like Lay into the poster boy of corporate greed? To put it differently, why do God-loving, morally upright leaders slowly become God-ignoring, morally corrupt leaders?

That is the question that keeps jumping at our face every time we read, hear, or see another Christian leader falling from grace. We cannot afford to blissfully ignore this question. We cannot pretend that it is irrelevant to us.

Six danger zones for leaders

The issue of Christian leader derailment is a perennial issue that will stay with us simply because Christian leaders are not infallible. That is what the doctrine of indwelling sin warns us, which we will examine in much greater depth in subsequent chapters. As they say, the heart of the problem is the problem of the heart.

Every single time we hear a highly respected Christian leader falling from grace, the proper response should be fear and trembling before God, for we are confronted yet again with the ugly reality of indwelling sin. Fear and trembling, yes. Surprised and shocked, no.

More generally speaking, the issue of leadership failures is somewhat a nascent topic in scholarly research. The field of organizational leadership has long been dominated by studies that have been built on a deeply held assumption that leaders are always morally good, and that their decisions and actions always benefit their constituents and organizations.

The deficit of scholarly attention in the area of destructive leadership is perplexing considering the ubiquity of blatantly corrupt leadership and their disastrous outcomes in contemporary organizations. It is therefore sobering to see that against the backdrop of an ongoing preoccupation with the heroic leadership paradigm, rigorous leadership studies that examine toxic leadership began around a decade ago and are on the increase (for a fuller discussion on the issue of destructive leadership, see Sendjaya, 2015).

The box below outlines some of the most pervasive areas where sin rears its ugly head at leaders. There are plenty of good resources that have been written on each of those issues, and there is no need to repeat them here. Leaders would be wise to avail themselves of these resources.

Common areas of leadership failures

1 Financial: Committing into decisions and actions that are motivated by personal financial gain
2 Relational: Building intimate relationships with someone of the opposite sex who is not a spouse or sibling
3 Sexual: Accessing materials that are pornographic in nature, particularly through social and electronic media, which lead into actionable habits

4 Intellectual: Thinking of self as the smartest and wisest, hence others' opinions and advice useful only for enlisting support

5 Emotional: Being easily defensive when criticized, angry when challenged, or evasive when shown weakness

6 Volitional: Having an inflated sense of entitlement, wanting to have the final say in everything, and thinking that they are irreplaceable

It's an inside job

If you are an avid reader of leadership, you would know that the overwhelming majority of leadership books claim with a varying degree of authority that the biggest threats to your leadership come from sources external to you, such as tectonic shifts in geo-politics, disruptive technologies, climate change, experience-based economy, etc. Indeed these external threats are occurring at a steady pace. They will render even high-performing leaders redundant if they do not out-stretch their current skillsets.

However, while it is important to advise leaders to be agile and adaptive to these significant and long-term changes, we will be remiss if we ignore a far greater danger that presents itself to us, not from outside of us but within us. The biblical teaching of the indwelling sin tells us that what cripples otherwise spiritually and emotionally capable leaders is always an inside job. The very thing that turns an effective leader into a destructive one runs through their hearts.

The greatest enemy of every leader is their own self. The oft-quoted adage still rings very true: 'We have met the enemy and once again, he is us.' Perhaps no one has learned that truth in a more powerful way than Aleksandr Solzhenitsyn (1973, pp. 615–616), a survivor of Stalin's Gulag in the 20th century:

> In my most evil moments I was convinced that I was doing good, and I was well supplied with systematic arguments. It was only when I lay there on rotting prison straw that I sensed within myself the first stirrings of good. Gradually it was disclosed to

me that the line separating good and evil passes not through states, nor between classes, nor between political parties either, but right through every human heart, and through all human hearts. This line shifts. Inside us, it oscillates with the years. Even within hearts overwhelmed by evil, one small bridge-head of good is retained; and even in the best of all hearts, there remains a small corner of evil.

We cannot leave that small corner of evil in our hearts unguarded. In the next section, we will illuminate that corner by paying a closer attention to the notion of self.

Discussions around preoccupation with self is so pervasive in both academic and popular circles. Scholars have studied with scientific rigor and precision many empirically valid constructs that relate to self. Here is a dozen of such examples (for a more academic treatment on these constructs, see Vignoles, Regalia, Manzi, Golledge, & Scabini, 2006). Drawing on the literature, I have provided below simple definitions for each construct to help us grasp their respective locus:

1 self-concept (an overall idea we have about who we are physically, emotionally, socially, spiritually, etc.),
2 self-esteem (a sense of one's value or worth),
3 self-image (perception of self that may not necessarily align with reality),
4 self-efficacy (the belief in one's ability to succeed at certain tasks),
5 self-confidence (trust in one's ability to engage successfully with the world),
6 self-awareness (understanding of one's own thoughts, feelings, behaviors, and traits),
7 self-knowledge (the self within a context so as to define the self),
8 self-actualization (realization of one's creative, intellectual, or social potential),
9 self-expression (enactment of valued identities),

10   self-coherence (a sense of wholeness across a set of identities),

11   self-continuity (a sense of wholeness across time), and

12   self-distinctiveness (a sense of uniqueness relative to others).

Underlying this fixation with self is the assumption that it can be improved or enhanced. However, as the arguments in this chapter and the rest of the book will show, the focus on self as the solution to leadership success is perhaps rather misguided because the self is in and of itself the epicenter of the problem. It is the ground zero of the catastrophic and multifaceted issues we have within and around us. The most fundamental reason why we experience envy, anxiety, shame, guilt, or burnout at work has more to do with the absence of the right understanding of self than the lack of coping mechanism skills.

■ The unholy trinity

To understand self correctly, we need to be fully aware about three things about human nature. We are created, limited, and polluted human beings; that is why we need to be saved from ourselves. First, we are created in the image of God, but that image of God has been marred with sin. Second, unlike God the Creator whose wisdom and power are limitless, we are limited creatures who are fond of acting like god. We think we are entitled to do whatever we like using whatever means we love whenever we want it. It is indeed easier to act like God than to love God. Finally, we are polluted human beings inside out, a predicament lamented by the ancient prophet Jeremiah, 'The heart is deceitful above all things, and desperately sick; who can understand it?' (Jeremiah 17:9).

Further scrutiny of this enemy within (i.e., the self) reveals that it never acts alone. It is not a solo operative. The self is always prone to the influences of three forces that through the ages have been relentless in their mission to bring down Christians: the flesh, the world, and the devil (Powlison, 2013). Together they form an alliance, the unholy trinity, which is briefly described below in relation to the individual leaders.

The flesh

The flesh does not merely refer to the physical body that we occupy; it rather points to an inclination in every faculty in our body that runs contrary to God. Our mind, emotions, and will are prone to the influence of the flesh that always seeks to put the *self* as the center of the universe.

We know that the authority of and power of the flesh over those of the God in our lives increase when the works of the flesh manifest in our lives. Extrapolating the list of the work of the flesh (Galatians 5:19–21) to the leadership context, we will have all sorts of counterproductive and destructive leadership behaviors such as sabotaging the work by procrastination, playing favorites to create division, backstabbing a colleague out of envy, theft, bullying, and sexual harassment.

The world

The self is also very susceptible to influences from *the world*, the second dark force in the unholy trinity. The world in this context refers to the anti-God value system and sociological influence that turn sinful behaviors into normal and legitimate behaviors.

Parents who are obsessed with academic or professional achievement will instil in their children the importance of attaining and retaining top spots in every endeavor using every means possible. If achievement is the familial or cultural idol that the children are brought up in, more likely than not, they will ascend to those places of power and influence at the exclusion of others. Workaholism becomes a standard work pattern given the increasing demands and pressures, leading into depression and burnouts experienced by countless corporate leaders.

Apart from our upbringing by parents, other influences such as interactions with friends, education by teachers, consumptions of social media, etc. converge and shape us to be the person we are today. The classic rendering of Romans 12:2 by Phillips (1956) is spot on. 'Don't let the world around you squeeze you into its own mould.' It remains a perpetual choice for Christian leaders whether they will allow God to remold them from within.

The devil

The devil is the third player, representing the spiritual or demono-logical influence above the leader whose accumulated wisdom in bringing down leaders over thousands of years has been legendary. He has been described quite eloquently as 'an active enemy [that] craves, schemes, lies, tempts, deceives, enslaves, accuses . . . and murders . . . The enemy minds you, finds you, wines and dines you, blinds you, binds you, and finally grinds you' (Powlison, 2013, p. 38).

The harmony with which the three dark forces above work together is quite an art form. It is intricate, elusive, and lethal. It injects us with a burgeoning amount of perceived sense of import-ance and entitlements that makes us feel we are superior to the average human being.

We tell ourselves that we are different because we are smarter and stronger, hence we deserve more than the rest. We believe that nothing can stop us from becoming what we want. We think that we are immune from the danger of temptations and sins.

The mutated self is altered so significantly that it is no longer rec-ognizable even from those who are close to us. Whenever popular business press picks up a story of derailed corporate leaders who have covered up their mischiefs over the years, they typically include interviews of the leaders' significant others for comments. Often the interview would include remarks of a downtrodden spouse who lamented to the guilty, 'You've changed so much I don't know you anymore. You are not the person I married three decades ago!'

The manifestations of this mutated self vary, but there are at least six emerging attitudes that the flesh, the world, and the devil grad-ually but surely change us into. As shown in Figure 1.1, the six attitudes are self-rule, self-centered, self-satisfied, self-confident, self-righteous, and self-sufficient.

These are not foreign concepts to us, simply because we have first-hand experiences with each and every single one of them. At the subconscious level, we tend to think that there are only five people in the world we care about: 'I, me, my, mine, myself'. Our intuitive pattern of thinking or the decision-making process is often, 'What's in it for me?'

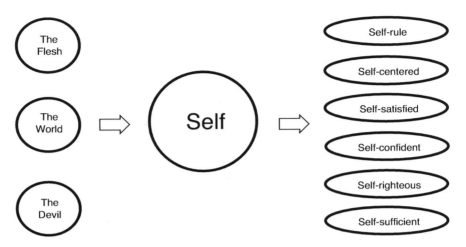

Figure 1.1 The origin and manifestation of sinful self

▓ Sinners with glorified titles

Leadership research suggests that enhancing self-efficacy is a primary means to develop leaders. Boosting leaders' self-efficacy to increase leadership effectiveness is sort of a paradigmatic position in the leadership development literature.

That may sound like a positive thing until we are confronted with the fact that *the self* is the main problem, as delineated above. Leaders who have developed higher self-efficacy can easily turn into insecure overachievers or bullying tyrants (or both) precisely because of their sinful self.

That is why the gospel matters. That is why leadership should never be detached from the gospel.

At the core of leaders' fall from grace is their complete ignorance of or unbelief in the gospel. Competencies might take leaders to the top, but without the gospel, leaders will not be built to last, no matter how effective and efficient they appear in the beginning.

What is the gospel? Simply put, the gospel is the good news that God is renewing all things in creation through the life, death, and resurrection of Jesus Christ. To say that the definition really packs a punch would be a gross understatement. Charles Hodge, a 19th century Princeton University theologian, once remarked that, 'The gospel is so simple that small children can understand it, and it is so profound that studies by the wisest theologians will never exhaust its riches.'

As a leadership professor in a business school, I am very mindful that there are many scientifically-rigorous strategies and evidence-based practices that can help leaders to navigate the treacherous path of leadership. But the best leadership strategies and practices that science can produce will *not* help leaders deal with the always-present temptations of power, comfort, approval, control, super-iority, and independence.

How is the gospel relevant to every leader of all shapes and sizes? The gospel shows the futility of appealing to one's self-efficacy, which would invariably leads to hubris when the individual is successful and despair when the individual fails.

In the final analysis, leaders are merely sinners with glorified titles. Even redeemed sinners are always prone to succumb into temptations this side of heaven. It goes without saying that business schools do not teach us this important truth.

Reforming the leader in you

The gospel shows that leaders are first and foremost sinners in need of a Savior. The gospel then prompts them to look to, rely on, and rest in Christ rather than their MBA, experiential wisdom, or investment portfolio.

That is why the most important and urgent need in leader-ship development today is not training, mentoring, or coaching. Spiritually dead leaders will remain dead after hours of training, mentoring, or coaching. They are not merely prone to sin or tempted to sin. Rather, they are dead in their sins. As such, all the improvements they make will make them more effective, authentic, and ethical leaders who remain dead spiritually. What leaders need therefore is not to be retooled, but to be resurrected. They need to be raised up to new life in Christ, lest we merely amuse ourselves to death.

There is only so much leadership development can do to help leaders guard their hearts. More broadly speaking, Christian author D.L. Moody was cognizant of the limitation of education when he famously remarked: 'If you come across a boy who's stealing nuts and bolts from a railway track, and you want to change him, and send him to college, at the end of his education he'll steal the whole railway track.' In fact, had it not been for the restraining common grace of God, all forms of leadership development would only facilitate the creation of civilized corporate sociopaths.

It does not mean that every leadership development endeavors will create toxic leaders, for that would be absurd. My point is without the gospel, leaders will not have a resource that is both robust and significant to help them deal with their dark side.

Underpinning each chapter in the book is the central argument that leaders need to be perpetually reformed in order to align with the gospel of Jesus Christ. Specifically, individual leaders need to be re-formed.

I am mindfully aware that leadership should be best understood as a relational dynamic among leaders and followers in specific context towards a specific purpose. In other words, leadership is not just about the leader but also followers and the context. However, if we ever hope for leadership to be reformed, we need to start with the individual leaders.

The theme of 'reforming leadership' is derived from the central story of the Scripture that God took the initiative on behalf of his creation who cannot help themselves to save and make them anew in Christ Jesus.

A bit of history might be warranted here to appreciate the context. The call to always reform ourselves and our social order was first articulated most clearly by the Reformers. In 1674 Jodocus van Lodenstein, a key figure in the Dutch Second Reformation, first wrote the importance of pursuing continual reformation in the lives and practices of the people of God (Horton, 2012, p. 120): 'The church is reformed, and always in need of being reformed according to the word of God' (or in Latin, *ecclesia reformata, semper reformanda secundum verbi Dei*).

Note the standard and manner of the reformation captured in the statement. The people of God are being reformed for the purpose of aligning them with the word of God, *not* the latest scientific breakthrough or defining spirit of our age. That is precisely why the rallying cry of the Reformers is '*ad fontes*', or back to the sources, not forward to today's megatrends. God's people can only progress to carry out their mission if they stay true to their original intent and design. Importantly, they cannot actively reform themselves. They need to be passively reformed through the external agency of God who moves through his spirit bringing us back to the thing of first importance, the gospel of Christ Jesus.

The need to continually be reformed makes a perfect sense given that in this fallen world, every nook and cranny of the created order is subjected to an ever-present and ever-increasing entropy. It is not just our cars that squeak and rattle, but organizations and their leaders too. Nearly 90% of Fortune 500 companies in the 1960s are no longer around today. The statistics are not much different for the church, as the Westminster divines prewarned us matter-of-factly that 'the purest Churches under heaven are subject both to mixture and error; and some have so degenerated, as to become no Churches of Christ, but synagogues of Satan.'

As early as the 1st century, the apostle Paul already faced leadership issues at the church of Corinth. Personality cult deeply divided members of the church based on their idolized leaders, rendering the local church leaders incapable of dealing with a garden variety of internal issues (e.g., individual(s) who get drunk at the holy communion, sleep with stepmothers, run to court with lawsuits at the drop of a hat rather than resolving minor disputes in an informal and amicable way).

Leaders are in need of being continually reformed indeed. Only then can we ever hope that they can reform the social structure they find themselves in. Drawing on the sermon of Puritan preacher Thomas Case to the English house of Commons in 1641, Wolterstorff (1983, p. 9) highlights the need to reform our institutions – the church, school, university, city, government, business, and so forth – because 'every plant that my heavenly Father has not planted will be rooted up' (Matthew 15:13):

> Clearly his assumption is that social structures are not something natural. They are not the reflection of true human nature. They are the result of human decision, and being made by us, they can be altered by us. Indeed, they *must* be altered, for they are fallen, corrupt. The structures *themselves* are corrupt and in need of reform, not only the persons who exist within these structures [italics original].

■ Why another leadership book

As insinuated above, the gospel is like *the* flashlight that illuminates the slippery path of leadership. It is absolutely critical to our understanding of leadership, yet rigorous works that examine the link between the gospel and leadership are almost non-existent.

The purpose of this book therefore is to employ the gospel-centered framework as a sensemaking tool to re-examine leadership and re-form leaders. Specifically, it integrates the biblical and scholarly perspectives to look at five areas of personal leadership effectiveness, namely desire, identity, dignity, motive, and ambition.

Why these five areas? Technically speaking, they are part of what psychologists would call 'individual differences', enduring psychological features that distinguish them from one another and shape each individual's sense of self and behaviors. Leaders may vary in their desire, identity, dignity, motive, and ambition – all of which would affect how and why they lead. There are traits that might be less malleable (e.g., race, culture), but by the grace of God, these five traits can be re-shaped by the gospel.

The other premise this book is built on is that effective leadership starts with leading self. Those who cannot lead themselves will struggle to lead other people, let alone the organization and the community at large. To change the world, one needs to start with changing one's self or more precisely, allowing one's self be changed by the gospel.

As such, this book is relevant for both Christian leaders and non-Christian leaders who long to see deep and lasting changes in the way they lead themselves. The materials in this book grew from the leadership workshops that I delivered to executives across faith-based organizations (e.g., churches, universities, schools, charity) and non-faith-based organizations in transportation, health care, and governmental, and non-governmental sectors.

That is why it is not a typical leadership book.

You will not find a systematic or critical review of leadership theories, approaches, or models in this book. Scientific studies on leadership have produced more than sixty leadership theory domains over the last six decades (Dinh et al., 2014). While you will encounter some of these theories in the pages that follow, the best articulation and discussion of these theories are found in many peer-reviewed academic journal articles.

The second thing you will not find is a complete biblical theology of leadership from the whole Scripture, or an exegesis of certain passages in relation to leadership. Granted this book draws on the biblical worldview to reinterpret key leadership topics, but it is not a full-blown theological treatise of leadership.

Finally, this book does not seek to cover a set of leadership competencies for the 21st century, digital economy, or disruptive organizations. An overwhelming majority of leadership books choose to focus on this subject. There are a few knowledge, skills, and abilities (cf. the KSA framework of leadership development) discussed in the book, but the central focus of this book lies in the ontological *being* of the leader.

What I mean by *being* is the essence of who we really are. People talk about character, conviction, core purpose sense of meaning, etc. when they have in-depth conversations about who they are.

This book is about leadership *being*. Specifically it is about leadership desire, identity, dignity, motive, and ambition. The focus on *being* is deliberate because leadership flows out of being. To be a leader is not a matter of simply choosing which leadership style suits my personality or the organizational culture. Leadership is a natural extension of who we are. *Being a leader* is a much more important element in the leadership equation relative to *doing leadership*.

Being is typically contrasted with *doing* (think about task-oriented skills such as strategic thinking or project management and people-oriented competencies such as conflict resolution or team building). *Doing* (i.e., skills and competencies) easily become obsolete particularly in this era of perpetual renewal and accelerated change; *being* (i.e., character and conviction) is considerably more stable, and difficult to instil.

The preoccupation with *doing* is unfortunate because it should not be the basis for defining who one is. There is a reason why we are called human beings rather than human doings. We are not our achievements. We are not our roles. Our worth lies in who we are as human beings who are created in the very image of the Creator God.

The book is structured around the five aforementioned areas of individual leadership differences, i.e., desire, identity, dignity, motive, and ambition.

Leadership desire is about what we love.
Leadership identity is about how we view ourselves.
Leadership dignity is about how we value performance.
Leadership motive is about whom we care.
Leadership ambition is about why we lead.

The chapters that follow feature vignettes, case studies, stories, and practical examples from the contemporary world and the Scripture to illustrate key points. There are questions and points for reflection to help apply the lessons learned to their individual contexts.

Chapter 2 traces the origin of six idolatrous desires within leaders to their sinful nature and how those six desires cripple them. The theme of idolatry is pervasive in the Scripture, and it is very useful in understanding why leaders do what they do not want to do. The patterns and examples of how these idolatrous desires in leaders' personal and professional lives are discussed.

Chapter 3 draws on organizational identity literature to introduce the notion of 'leading servants' as a personal leadership identity (as opposed to 'servant leaders'). This is not a compromise between the idea of 'powerful leader' that the world expects and 'humble servant' that God expects because the gospel provides a solid foundation for leaders to embrace both identities.

Chapter 4 sheds light on how leaders can be high-performing without worshiping the god of performance. Self-made performance treadmills have claimed too many leaders, novice and seasoned alike. In this chapter, I discuss how the gospel enables the fluid dynamic between leadership being (being accepted as we are in Christ) and leadership doing (performing highly for Christ).

Chapter 5 discusses the leadership dilemma of living for people's approval. Fear of man is often the Achilles heel of many leaders, but is it always a bad idea to try to please the very individuals we lead? The gospel offers a solution to this dilemma that is radically different from secular psychology, liberating leaders from the tyranny of people's opinions so they can genuinely receive compliments without pride, take criticism without bitterness, affirm others in earnest, and speak the truth in love.

Chapter 6 deals with our ambivalent feelings towards ambition. Too little or too much ambition is typically met with a frown. Drawing on the eschatological vision of shalom, I outline how the gospel both sanctifies and saturates leaders' ambition. This awareness will enable them to lead with creative tension to change the world back in line with the initial design.

Finally, Chapter 7 summarizes the book by highlighting the slow, gradual process of decline when leaders ignore the gospel. In particular there are five distinct patterns in relation to the preceding chapters, that is when leaders' desire to lead does not come *from Christ*, their identity not secure *in Christ*, their dignity is not aligned *with Christ*, their motive is not oriented *towards Christ*, and their ambition is not set *for* Christ.

References

Bryce, R. (2003). *Pipe dreams: Greed, ego, and the death of Enron*. New York: Public Affairs.

Cruver, B. (2003). *Enron: Anatomy of greed* (p. 10). London: Arrow Books.

Dinh, J. E., Lord, R. G., Gardner, W. L., Meuser, J. D., Liden, R. C., & Hu, J. (2014). Leadership theory and research in the new millennium: Current theoretical trends and changing perspectives. *The Leadership Quarterly*, 25(1), 36–62.

Fusaro, P. C., & Miller, R. M. (2002). *What went wrong at Enron*. Hoboken: John Wiley.

Horton, M. (2012). Reformed and always reforming. In R. S. Clark & J. E. Kim (Eds.), *Always reformed: Essays in honor of W. Robert Godfrey*. Westminster Seminary California.

McLean, B., & Elkind, P. (2003). *The smartest guys in the room: The amazing rise and scandalous fall of Enron*. New York: Portfolio.

Phillips, J. B. (1956). *New Testament Christianity*. London: Hodder and Stoughton.

Powlison, D. (2013). Revisiting idols of the heart and vanity fair. *Journal of Biblical Counseling*, 27(3), 37–68.

Sendjaya, S. (2015). *Personal and organizational excellence through servant leadership*. Springer International.

Solzhenitsyn, A. (1973). *The gulag archipelago: 1918–1956* (Vol. 2, pp. 615–616). New York: Harper and Row.

Swartz, M. (2003). *Power failure: The rise & fall of Enron*. London: Aurum Press.

Vignoles, V. L., Regalia, C., Manzi, C., Golledge, J., & Scabini, E. (2006). Beyond self-esteem: Influence of multiple motives on identity construction. *Journal of Personality and Social Psychology*, 90, 308–333.

Wolterstorff, N. (1983). *Until justice and peace embrace: The Kuyper lectures for 1981 delivered at the Free University of Amsterdam*. Grand Rapids, MI: W.B. Eerdmans.

2

Leadership and the psychology of desire

'The human heart is a perpetual factory of idols . . .
Every one of us is, from his mother's womb,
expert in inventing idols.'
(*Calvin, Institutes, Book 1, 11:108*)

As delineated in the previous chapter, if indeed we are our own worst enemy, and the self has been shaped and even corrupted by the unholy trinity, the task of understanding ourselves more intelligently, critically, and thoroughly can never be understated. This is particularly true if we aspire to or are in the position of leadership. To paraphrase Socrates, a leader with an unexamined heart is not worth following.

The most logical place to start examining ourselves is our desires. Examining the psychology of our desires is critical for at least three reasons. First, every individual by nature has desires, and since they often conflict with each other, they need to be regulated. We might recognize desires with different terms, i.e., wishes, longings, preferences, hopes, and expectations. These desires can be biological or existential, but both must be fulfilled in order for us to be able to function normally in the society, in fact to survive.

Biological desires are quite straightforward. When our bodies tell us to rehydrate, we go and find a glass of water to quench our thirst. Existential desires are more complex as they are manifested through our life choices and priorities, career trajectories, preferred way of interacting with people, etc. The desires to love and be loved, to be in control, to be significant, and to be successful are some of the deepest longings of hearts that must be met from the minute we were born into this world. These innate desires will continuously be shaped by contextual influences we are exposed to throughout our lives.

While our desires are often benign and functional, there are instances where even our most basic desires run counter with each other. A most poignant biblical example comes from Jesus, the Son of Man, who during his earthly ministry experienced the onslaught of the devil in the area of desire. After fasting for forty days and forty nights, he was understandably famished. The devil tempted him to turn the stones lying nearby into loaves of bread (cf. Matthew 4:1–11).

The reason Jesus resisted the devil's temptation was not because he was immune from the physiology of hunger, nor because he thought that experiencing hunger was sinful. Jesus did not do what the devil asked him because he refused to be mastered by his desires, and chose to submit to a higher desire, which is to obey his heavenly Father who in his perfect will and timing satisfies his temporal desire of food. Later in the same passage, we are told that the angels were ministering to him, replenishing his body.

The second reason why it is important for us to understand our desire to grasp who we really are is because our desires shape our behaviors. Scholarly research on desire shows that our desires emerge at our subconscious level when 'reward-processing centers in midbrain regions (e.g., ventral striatum) evaluate external stimuli (or mental images thereof) against the backdrop of internal need stages and an individual's learning history)' (Hofmann, Kotabe, Vohs, & Baumeister, 2015, p. 64). In plain English, it means that our desires trigger impulsive and habitual responses that might occur outside of our conscious awareness. As the desired stimulus around us gains access to our consciousness, our thoughts and behaviors will be deeply affected.

Long before scientists formulated that neural pathway of desire, Jesus had the foresight on the salience of desire in the formation of self. When he called his first disciples, he perceptively asked,

'What do you want?' or, as another translation renders it, 'What are you seeking for?' (John 1:38). Interestingly, that is not an isolated incident, for different variants of that question appear in the four Gospels, i.e., around the issue of love, wish, want, and passion. Jesus understands that our desire has a pull factor that is much stronger than the push factor of our cognition, as the following remark alludes to (Smith, 2009, p. 32):

> Being a disciple of Jesus is not primarily a matter of getting the right ideas and doctrines and beliefs into your head in order to guarantee proper behavior rather, it's a matter of being the kind of person who loves rightly – who loves God and neighbor and is oriented to the world by the primacy of that love.

Finally, the third reason why we need to understand our desires is the perceived sense of importance that typically accompanies leadership can easily intensify our desires. There are a few desires associated with leadership roles, i.e., desire to control or achieve, to be praised or respected, for approval or attention. These desires are typically amplified in a leader's life commensurate with the amount of power and influence they exert. The more powerful they are, the more intense these desires. Many are willing to walk the treacherous path of leadership because of their inner longing towards them.

Morally neutral desires

It is important to highlight that leaders' desires to be in control, appreciated, and respected are morally neutral. They are part and parcel of what it means to be human. These natural affections not only constitute an ingrained part of humanity, but they also set us apart from other created beings.

Unlike lower forms of created beings, humans are capable of telling the difference between blessing and curse, right and wrong. What makes us human is our preference towards health over sickness, financial independence over poverty, happy family over miserable one, and so forth. That is precisely why we take calculated risks time and again to attain those things.

Contextualizing it for leaders, it is quite normal for leaders to have a drive to lead or a passion for a cause. Take, for example, the drive to lead. Research on trait theories of leadership shows that individuals who aspire to be leaders have a strong drive to lead (Kirkpatrick & Locke, 1991). A constellation of traits grouped under the drive to lead (e.g., energy, initiative, tenacity) has been singled out as a strong predictor of successful performance.

Providentially, that is aligned with the biblical characteristics for church elders, that is one must have an aspiration to the office of overseer (1 Timothy 3:1). The apostle Paul seemed to suggest that leaders without a desire to lead should not bother to apply in the first place.

Granted the drive to lead may not necessarily imply a hunger for power as an end in itself. But the line between the two can quickly become quite blurry as the span of control one has increases. Corporations all over the world are filled with leaders whose sole ambition is to gain more power, money, status (or all of them), leading them to all sorts of unethical and unlawful behaviors. In other words, the natural desire to lead gradually turns into the ruling desire to always be in control. The natural desire that frees us to fulfil our God-given potentials morphs into a sinful desire that enslaves us.

Christian leaders need to be cautious of their deep desires because of their inherent danger. Why do seemingly innocent desires become a critical failure factor for leaders? Because these desires can be out of order and inordinate.

▓ Out of order and out of control desires

Early church father Saint Augustine (354–430) coined the phrase 'disordered love' to describe a desire that is out of its rightful order. We were created to love God first and foremost, which is why we have a heart-shaped vacuum that can only be filled by God. Our love is disordered when it seeks happiness in the ephemeral and finite objects in the created world rather than the eternal and infinite Creator God. The biggest problem with the attempts to satisfy one's desire in these temporary things is that they are metaphysically incapable of meaningfully satisfying the individual.

Rather than giving them true happiness, all desires other than a desire towards God will crush the person with self-dwindling expectations. This reasoning lies behind his oft-quoted line, 'O Lord, Thou has made us for Thyself, and our spirits are restless [unhappy] until they rest in Thee' (Augustine & Watts, 1979, Book I, 1.1). C.S. Lewis (1968, p. 136) echoed this sentiment when he remarked, 'If I find in myself a desire which no experience in this world can satisfy, the most probable explanation is that I was made for another world.'

The second reason why our desires are enslaving us is because they can become out of control. Theologian John Calvin (*Institutes*, ed. Battles, p. 604) wrote of the nature of idolatry as follows: 'we teach that all human desires are evil, and charge them with sin – not in that they are natural but because they are inordinate.' Of course, there are many desires that are evil in and of themselves; often they are punishable by law. The desire to steal the property of others, for example, falls into this category. However, as intimated above, an overwhelming majority of our desires are morally neutral.

As such, the object of our desire is often neutral, but it is the primacy of our desire that makes it lethal. To put it differently, the danger with our desires is not in our pursuit of them, but in being consumed by them. Pursuing our desires makes us human, pursuing them above all else makes us diabolical. There is nothing inherently wrong with wanting to have peer recognition or public acclaim, but wanting it too excessively will tempt leaders to use any means necessary to achieve that end. This brings us to the important concept of idolatry.

Idolatrous desires

Broadly defined, idolatry is turning an otherwise morally good and legitimate desire into an ultimate and ruling desire of our lives. In so doing, when we engage in idolatry we launch a *coup d'état*, dethroning the Creator God from his rightful place as ruler of our lives and installing our desires as the new illegitimate ruler. The Idol.

Idolatry is perhaps the most powerful framework from which leaders can guard their own hearts. The extent to which Christian leaders can be effective depends on their awareness of two things: Their idolatrous hearts and their need of the gospel. To put it differently, every leader has idolatrous desires, and the only hope they have to deal with those lethal desires is the gospel of Jesus Christ.

Granted that is a bold thesis statement, and as such a short disclaimer is perhaps warranted. I am acutely aware that this position will provoke either a hearty amen or outright contempt. If yours is the latter, I hope that you can muster patience large enough to continue reading this chapter, indulging me while I am unpacking it in the rest of this chapter.

Idolatry in the Bible

An old maxim attributed to P.T. Forsyth says that 'the first duty of every soul is to find not its freedom but its Master.' We are created to worship something or someone at any given time. We need to live our lives in worship of one thing that is greater than ourselves. We may call it with different names – mission, vision, strategic direction, goal, objective, passion – but whatever captures our desire will demand sacrifices of our time and energy. The more important these greater-than-self things are, the more we are willing to exert our personal resources to attain and retain them.

In other words, we live to worship them. Rather than worshipping the Creator God as the source of our happiness, meaning, and purpose, we are worshipping god-substitutes or idols. The principle is succinctly put as follows, 'Whatever your heart clings to or relies upon, that is your god' (Beale, 2008, p. 6).

Idolatrous desire represents a key framework through which sin is viewed in the Bible and as such is pervasively discussed as a most common human problem in both the Old and New Testament. A contemporary understanding of the link between idolatry and sin is provided by Keller (2008, p. 162):

> The primary way to define sin [in the Bible] is not just the doing of bad things, but the making of good things into ultimate things. It is seeking to establish a sense of self by making something else more central to your significance, purpose and happiness than your relationship to God.

In the Old Testament, Israel was noted in the Bible as an idol-worshipping nation, idols that were spiritually empty, thus bearing resemblance to the spiritual emptiness of their idols (2 Kings 17:15–16 and Jeremiah 2:5). In his commentary on idolatry, Brueggemann (1998, p. 34) wrote, 'One takes on the character of the god one follows . . . We become like the god we serve. Pursue a bubble and become a bubble.'

Even more compelling is the unison with which the writers, Paul, Peter, John, James, highlighted the lethal force of idolatrous cravings or lust of the flesh as a summary of what is wrong with human beings (cf. Galatians 5:16; Ephesians 2:3; 1 Peter 2:11, 4:2; 1 John 2:16; James 1:14). Of particular note is the way Paul defined idolatry in his letter to the Romans: 'They exchanged the truth about God for a lie and worshiped and served the creature rather than the Creator, who is blessed forever!' (Romans 1:25).

Another curious scriptural evidence of the pervasiveness of idolatry is found in the first letter written by the apostle John. The apostle John chose to end a 105-verse treatment on how to have a dynamic life in Jesus Christ with these seemingly poor-fitting words, "Beloved children, keep yourselves from idols" (1 John 5:21). Commenting on this verse, Powlison (1995, p. 35) wrote:

> John's last line properly leaves us with that most basic question which God continually poses to each human heart. Has something or someone besides Jesus the Christ taken title to your heart's trust, preoccupation, loyalty, service, fear and delight? It is a question bearing on the immediate motivation for one's behavior, thoughts, and feelings. In the Bible's conceptualization, the motivation question is the lordship question. Who or what "rules" my behavior, the Lord or a substitute? The undesirable answers to this question – answers which inform our understanding of the "idolatry" we are to avoid – are most graphically presented in 1 John 2:15–17, 3 :7–10, 4 :1–6, and 5:19.

These idols are internal and imaginary, not external and physical. In the ancient Greco-Roman world, the Greeks worshipped their territorial gods quite intensely (Aphrodite, the goddess of beauty;

Artemis, the goddess of fertility; Ares, the god of war; Hephaestus, the god of craftsmanship). The practice of idol-worship however continues to live on until today. We too are idol-worshippers. In the modern world, we worship different gods, performing different services, making different sacrifices, and doing it all in different temples. The link between ancient and contemporary cultures is clearly explained below (Keller, 2009, pp. xi–xii):

> Our contemporary society is not fundamentally different from these ancient ones. Each culture is dominated by its own set of idols. Each has its 'priesthoods,' its totems and rituals. Each one has its shrines – whether office towers, spas and gyms, studios, or stadiums – where sacrifices must be made in order to procure the blessings of the good life and ward off disaster. What are the gods of beauty, power, money, and achievement but these same things that have assumed mythic proportions in our individual lives and in our society?
>
> We may not physically kneel before the statue of Aphrodite, but many young women today are driven into depression and eating disorders by an obsessive concern over their body image. We may not actually burn incense to Artemis, but when money and career are raised to cosmic proportions, we perform a kind of child sacrifice, neglecting family and community to achieve a higher place in business and gain more wealth and prestige.

The lessons for leaders are quite obvious. Think about how we approach our career, for example. To meticulously plan for career success is a commendable thing, but to make it our prime goal in life such that we sacrifice our spouses and children would engage us in idolatrous worship to Mammon, the god of wealth (Keller, 2009). In doing so, we are no different from the ancient Greco-Roman people who worship their idols, making continuing sacrifices to procure blessings and remove curses. The priests (and sometimes, priestesses) are the larger-than-life CEOs who work in excess of fifty hours a week and think that work-life balance is for wimps. The shrines are corner offices in skyscrapers, and the rituals include daily briefings where executive decisions that involve countless stakeholders are made.

▮ Identifying and discerning idols

What I hope to accomplish in the remaining part of the chapter is twofold: Providing signposts for us to be able to identify our specific idols and unravelling the characteristics of these idols.

Idolatrous desires are complex. That is why it is such a pervasive theme throughout the entire Bible. Powlison (1995, p. 36) puts it as follows: 'If idolatry is the characteristic and summary of the OT word for our drift from God, then "desires" (*epithumiai*) is the characteristic and summary NT word for the same drift.'

If all of life is, as Luther's oft-quoted remark, repentance, it means that we should continually repent from the idols that take residence within us. For us to be able to repent more intelligently each time, we need to understand how these idols operate as they relate to leaders and leadership themes.

The best resource to discern our idols I will heartily recommend is Powlison's (2003) X-Ray questions, which help us identify the functional gods who control every area of our minds, emotions, attitudes, and actions. Sample questions include, 'What do you want, desire, crave, lust, and wish for? On your deathbed, what would sum up your life as worthwhile? What would make you feel rich, secure, and prosperous? What situations do you feel pressured or tense? What preoccupies or obsesses you?'

These heart-probing questions are relevant for leaders of all stripes; no doubt some questions resonate with us more than others. In order to make them more directly relevant to personal leadership development, I have adapted from Powlison's X-Ray question the following reflective questions for leaders, each followed by a short commentary.

▮ Seven idol-revealing leadership reflective questions

1   *What preoccupies your mind as leaders?*
    Where our thoughts drift effortlessly on autopilot when we are relaxed often indicates what we truly value in life. Think about the first 10 minutes when you wake up in the morning or the last 10 minutes before you doze off at night. Or think about what you habitually daydream during

lunch hour. The very things that occupy your mind when nothing urgent and/or important demands our attention reveal your idol. For leaders, what typically occupies their mind could be their career progress, their company IPO or stock price, or the relationship with their family members. Consulting firms and business schools regularly conduct studies around what CEOs think. Inside the minds of the CEOs are clues to identifying their idols.

2   *What do you strive to have throughout your career?*
While leadership is certainly a responsibility, the position often come with all sorts of perks and privileges. Left unchecked, it is fairly easy for leaders to be more concerned with their rights above their responsibilities. Countless leaders are craving for things like peer respect, an internal sense of achievement, status and prestige, financial wealth, multiple investment properties, or others. Idols promise security and pleasure apart from God. If you are banking on one thing above others to attain happiness, then that one thing could well be your idol.

3   *What would you protect at all cost?*
Those who have worked long and hard to secure a leadership position are typically not keen to let it go. This is a pervasive trend among the C-suite executives. If it becomes embedded in the corporate culture, it will easily trickle down to the lower management. For other leaders, perhaps it is not so much about their leadership position, but the approval of the public, respect of their boss, love of their spouse, access to a life of luxury, or freedom to make big decisions. Since idols engage the deepest emotions of our hearts, whatever you think essential for your survival or sanity might well be your idol.

4   *What makes you feel like a VIP?*
What is the one thing that you always mention or are eager to share in social gatherings? Do you always highlight your achievements, your company, your ministry, your investments, or something else? If you meet someone new or are introduced to someone, what description about

yourself would you wish the other person know after you say your name? What makes us feel like we significantly matter point to your idol.

5   *How do you justify your leadership decisions?*
This question does not refer to compliance with the law or corporate code, important as they are. Needless to say, Christian leaders must ensure that their actions are legally compliant. The question rather asks what makes your decisions ethically right or wrong. Are they driven by personal gain and loss (i.e., 'greed is good'), cost-and-benefit analysis ('the business of business is business'), public expectations and approval, internalized principles of ethics, or something else? Whatever drives your decisions says a lot about your idol.

6   *What triggers anxiety, stress, or anger in you?*
Think about your daily interactions with people at home, work, church, and elsewhere. What sort of comments make you annoyed and fumed? Which incidents make you flipped? Are there any topics that you set to be off limits even to your loved ones? Research on work-life conflicts show that for many executives, marital issues are major stressors. For others, it could be the perceived lack of acknowledgement from your boss, less than satisfactory team performance, or reduced sense of control of your work. Anything that makes you anxious, stressed, or angry might be your idol.

7   *Where do you turn for comfort or safety when things get tough?*
What we do when we try to escape the daily grind or medicate ourselves from the pain of disappointment may speak volume about our idols. This is particularly relevant for overworked leaders who are at the brink of burnout. Many find refuge in alcohol, video games, books, pornography, or food. Others find security in engaging in more work driven by the 'I-feel-guilty-when-I-am-relaxed' syndrome. Christian leaders may be able to recite by heart the first question from the Heidelberg Catechism, "What is your only comfort in life and death? That I am not my own, but belong – body and soul, in life and in death – to my faithful Savior, Jesus Christ." The reality is starkly different

however. When things get tough, their comfort is found in whiskey or online pornography instead. Our pattern of escape shows our idols.

Six motive idols

We have thus far discussed the link between leadership and idolatry, and strategies to identify the idols within the leaders' hearts. Next, we examine six primary idols that have salient individual effects in leaders. They provide the most basic explanation as to why leaders do what they do.

If we impose these primary idols on the iceberg metaphor, they will be found on the lower part of the iceberg, invisible to others and even to us. That is why they are called *motive* idols. The visible part of the iceberg is our reactionary emotions and actions. To shed light on the underlying reason why we are angry, envious, anxious, bitter, annoyed, or disgusted, we need to identify motive idols.

Table 2.1 outlines the six basic groupings of idols, namely power, approval, comfort, control, superiority, and independence, along with their respective correlates. It also serves as a summary of our discussions thus far in this chapter. Using the approach-avoidance framework (i.e., we are pleasure-seeking and pain-avoiding creatures), the table shows how each manifestation of sinful self and its corresponding idolatrous desire appear on the surface of the leaders' lives in terms of what they tend to seek and avoid. The last two columns show the ensuing typical problem behaviors and emotions of idol-worshipping leaders.

To continue using the Enron example, I will draw on Enron's former CEO Jeff Skilling to elucidate the above point. Shortly after getting hired by Ken Lay, Skilling developed a cut-throat corporate culture within Enron where only the fittest survive (Bryce, 2003; Fusaro & Miller, 2002).

He had a humongous sense of entitlement, convinced that he was the smartest guy in the company at any given time. He would dismiss anyone who disagreed with him as not bright enough to understand his idea. He continually undermined other energy companies using demeaning labels such as 'dinosaurs destined for extinction' (Cruver, 2003) and repeatedly claimed that Enron

Table 2.1 Six primary idolatrous desires and their manifestations and behavioral-emotional effects in leaders

Manifestations of Sinful Self	Idolatrous Desires	What I would seek: 'I'd be happy if I . . .'	What I would avoid: 'I'd collapse if I . . .'	Problem Behaviors	Problem Emotions
Self-rule	Power (success, winning, influence, work, achievement)	Perform beyond expectations such that I command respect from others, and people listen and obey me.	I did not do well or worse, fail. People will see me as weak, and I will feel humiliated.	User of people, driven, workaholic, strong and sharp façade outside but fragile and shallow inside	Irritated, angry, jealous
Self-centered	Approval (affirmation, love, relationship, family, dependence)	Am loved, approved, and / or respected by significant others; people need me.	Am not loved, approved, and / or respected by significant others, feel rejected.	Controlling, insecure, constantly and easily hurt by criticism, eager to please	Anxious, guilty, cowardly
Self-satisfied	Comfort (pleasure, privacy, freedom)	Perceive that my wishes and preferences are fulfilled (rights, privacy, freedom, quality of life).	Perceive that others interfere with my wishes and preferences.	Strong preference towards, or addiction to something	Demanding, frustrated

(Continued)

Table 2.1 (Continued)

Manifestations of Sinful Self	Idolatrous Desires	What I would seek: 'I'd be happy if I . . . '	What I would avoid: 'I'd collapse if I . . . '	Problem Behaviors	Problem Emotions
Self-confidence	Control (security, certainty, mastery)	Have certainty to be able to secure my future, to master my life in areas I deem important, and to do what I want to do.	Have no certainty about my future, sensing that things are happening outside my control, and other people tell me what to do.	Overbearing, patronizing, expecting compliance from others (and getting only grudging compliance at best)	Impatient, distrusting, shame
Self-righteous	Superiority (religion, ideology, image)	Feel that I am better than others in terms of opinion, morality, ideology, doctrine, or look.	Am being proven inferior to others in my opinion, morality, ideology, doctrine, or look.	Condescending, disdaining others who are different as inferior	Arrogant, disgusted, confrontative
Self-sufficient	Independence	Am completely capable and independent, don't need other people and don't have to care.	I depend on others or others depend on me, feel paranoid about my lack of independence.	Boastful, deviant, loner	Indifferent, detached

*Adapted from various works by Tim Keller, Timothy Lane, Paul Tripp, and David Powlison (see the reference list at the end of the chapter to see the titles of their work).

was going to bury the competition. His narcissistic tendency was best shown in his strategy to reproduce himself in others by hiring extremely competitive, single-minded MBAs who were willing to work eighty hours a week, a set of attributes which earned them membership of an elite tribe called 'Skillingites'.

Many would diagnose Skilling as a person showing high level of sub-clinical traits such as narcissism, Machiavellianism, and psychopathy, the three dark traits that are commonly found among self-absorbed, delusional, demanding, yet formidable and charismatic executives. From the idolatry framework, however, it is obvious that he exhibits extreme forms of idolatrous desires of power and control.

First, *power* idolatry is manifested in his operating assumption that the worth of his leadership and even his entire existence is derived from his competitive power to crash the other players in the industry and dominate the market share. This 'I am powerful therefore I am' mentality drove many reckless and unethical behaviors. Skilling had little regard towards rules both within and beyond the company. He repeatedly told his followers that because they are special, rules do not apply to them. Even accounting rules were considered obstacles that should be removed in order to achieve a greater level of success. Profit maximization was perceived to be an inherent part of doing good, and the stock market became the ultimate judge of right and wrong.

As with every idol, the idol of power also needs to be protected to be able to continue to give him a sense of self-worth. That explains why he orchestrated one of the biggest accounting scandals known in history and covered up losses by massaging the numbers in the company books.

The other motive idol that strongly drove Skilling was *control*. It led him to think that his significance is equal to the amount of control he has over other people. Skilling was notoriously known within the company as Darth Vader, 'a master of the energy universe who had the ability to control people's minds' (Cruver, 2003, p. 10). The dramaturgical efforts to portray himself as a mighty boss worthy of all allegiance and respect were quite intense. In company gatherings, he dressed as Darth Vader and referred to his traders as 'Storm Troopers'.

How idols operate: Four key patterns

As insinuated above, in order to be able to fight the enemy within, we need to have a good understanding of the patterns in which these idols operate within our hearts. What they could not accomplish much by frontal assaults to take our hearts captive they would have to accomplish by stealth. Many leaders are not aware of this clandestine operation, naively thinking they are in control of what they say and do whilst in reality they are being controlled by their idols. Below are four main patterns that are often operational in many leaders' lives.

1. Idols operate through fear and pride

When idols launch their covert attack, their preferred weapons of mass destruction are fear and pride. Fear and pride are primal emotions we are hardwired within. They are basic and instinctive emotions that trigger other emotions and behaviors as a means to survive or adapt to our surroundings. That is why I do not include fear and pride in the list of problem emotions in Table 2.1.

A closer reflection tells us the intricate link between these two emotions and our desires. We experience fear and pride if we have deficiency or surplus, respectively, of what we love. If leaders crave comfort, their fear is pain and poverty, and their pride is pleasure and opulence. If leaders seek approval, getting rejected will terrify them and getting praised will satisfy them. If leaders love pre-eminent status and respect, they dread the thought of being inferior to others and beam with pride for being superior to others.

As an illustration, think of a charismatic leader who is very talented and hardworking, yet arrogant and abrasive towards others. Oblivious to the work of idols in his hearts, he thinks that as a leader, he must have the final say in every decision in the organization and micro-manage its execution. Underlying his thoughts and behaviors is a nagging fear that the absence of his direct influence will result in a sub-optimum level of organizational performance, which in turn leads to the collapse of the organization. He deeply believes that 'only the paranoid survives', and that highly performing organizations is a non-negotiable for a vibrant economy.

While this fear might not be entirely irrational, it always manifests in a disproportionate amount.

Apart from fear, the other influence process mechanism often employed by idols is pride. The leader feels he cannot afford to lose face in front of the public if the organization performs at a mediocre level. Only lazy, weak, and uncivilized people are content with mediocre performance. He would do everything in his power to bring the organization to the next level of success, even if it means sacrificing his staff on the altar of growth and profit.

Note that fear and pride are also universal emotions that are experienced by every leader. If in God's providence, that leader becomes a Christian, will this unfounded fear and pride necessarily disappear? As is often the case, they would remain within the leader. They get baptized, and the emotions resurface in a religious version of fear and pride. The leader will fear the stern discipline from God (or at least the absence of blessings) if he does not put in his 110% into his organization, fully aware that everything that he does is now for the Lord.

What about pride? As a Christian, he now has a new conviction that the difference between sinners and himself is his unflinching ambition to excel at work as service to God. 'God helps those who help themselves, God's blessings upon me is proof that I am not like those unworthy sinners who are ungratefully lazy,' or so he thought.

Leaders should not take lightly the advice to guard their hearts, for everything they do flows from it. And they need the light of the gospel to be able to see how those dimmed corners of their hearts have been taken captive by fear and pride that their idols have surgically planted. Given the salience of fear and pride in the leaders' hearts, we will revisit them more in-depth in subsequent chapters. The issue of fear and pride will be discussed more in-depth in subsequent chapters.

2. Idols enhance our sense of entitlement

Becoming a leader typically magnifies one's sense of entitlement. Scholars commonly define psychological entitlement as the perception that one has a legitimate right to special treatment, regardless of one's deservingness. Examples of entitled leadership behaviors are as follows: Demanding respect without giving it to others, expecting praise and adulation but never showing appreciation to others, or requiring others to stay late in the office while leaving early.

Entitled leaders are oblivious of their own grandiose sense of entitlement. They would brush off any feedback that they behave like obnoxiously entitled individuals because they feel they have obtained every right to do so. They even feel 'morally licensed' in engaging in immoral or unethical behaviors.

Moral licensing theory posits that individuals may behave in morally questionable or ethically ambiguous behaviors after they perform some moral or ethical behaviors (Merritt, Effron, & Monin, 2010). Drawing on prior understanding on behavioral priming and moral regulation, researchers empirically showed using experimental studies that a prior good deed provides a 'license' for someone to do a bad deed. For example, volunteering in community work increases the tendency for people to allow themselves to omit additional income when completing their tax return.

In fact, a meta-analytic review of studies that compare a licensing condition with a control condition concludes that the magnitude of moral licensing effects on immoral, unethical, or problematic behaviors is quite significant (Blanken, van de Nen, & Zeelenberg, 2015). In an interesting study, researchers found that since purchasing green products affirms individuals' values of social responsibility and ethical consciousness, purchasing green products (as compared to purchasing conventional products) would establish moral credentials, which in turn would ironically license selfish and immoral behaviors, namely cheating and stealing (Mazar & Zhong, 2010).

Behind the insidious growth of leaders' sense of entitlement and moral licensing effects are the idols of power, approval, comfort, control, superiority, or independence. Think about comfort, for example. Nearly every other week we would read newspaper headlines on leaders who misuse taxpayers' money for extravagant travel and spending. A public officer in the US from the housing and urban development was found recently to break the law by spending $165,000 on office lounge furniture while claiming that homeless shelters should not be comfortable so that the poor will work harder to improve their life condition (Graham, 2019).

The harder and longer leaders have worked to attain the roles they occupy, the more they feel it's perfectly justifiable to engage in unethical or illegal behaviors that they otherwise would not do. Behind the leaders' pattern of reasoning, 'I just did good deed A, so now I can do bad deed B' is the efficient and effective work of idols. Like stealth aircrafts who can fly under the radar, idols' operation often does not register a reading on our tracking systems.

3.   One idol can manifest in different sins

The third pattern with which idols operate is that one dominant idol in our lives can take the form of multiple sins (Powlison, 2003). Let's take Judas Iscariot, for example. A cursory reading of his life, as depicted in the Scripture, would suggest that his life was driven by the love of money (i.e., power idolatry). In line with the oft-quoted biblical teaching that 'the love of money is a root for all sorts of evil' (1 Timothy 6:10), this lust for mammon entangled him in vicious cycles of diverse sins, namely lying, collusion, betrayal, and despair.

First, he lied to his teeth. He lodged a complaint to Jesus over the unwise use of very expensive ointment to anoint the feet of Jesus. Worth roughly one year's wages, he argued that it should have been sold and the money given to the poor. But such a theologically sound and politically correct argument can flow from a twisted motive. Judas never planned to help the poor; he was a thief, and selling the ointment afforded him the opportunity to have his way into the proceeds.

Second, he colluded with the religious leaders to capture Jesus. He was turned because of his love of mammon. Third, he betrayed Jesus to gain blood money and sealed it with a kiss on the cheek to mark Jesus in front of the Roman soldiers. Fourth, rather than repenting of his sins like Simon Peter, Judas was filled by despair.

The story of Judas is a sober reminder to every Christian leader that our intensive service in God's work and even proximity to God are not reliable indicators of faith in God himself. Three years of up close and personal encounters with Jesus meant that he had the finest teaching and most solid evidence he ever needed to follow the greatest leader alive, yet so inextricably entangled his heart was with craving for money.

The same idolatry of power-induced money is still at work in many Christian leaders, creating a barrage of creative manifestations of sins. Reflect on the following words and check if we can relate to any particular sin on the following list (Powlison, 2003, p. 152).

> Every one of the Ten Commandments – and more – can be broken by someone who loves and serves money. The craving for money and material possessions is an organizing theme for symptomatic sins as diverse as anxiety, theft, compulsive shopping, murder, jealousy, marital discord, a sense of inferiority or of superiority compared to others, sexual immorality that trades sex for material advantage, and so forth.

4. One sin is shaped by different idols

The fourth pattern is squarely the opposite, one dominant sin can be shaped by multiple idols (Powlison, 2003). Perhaps the most fitting biblical illustration for this pattern is Simon Peter. Over the years I have found that of all biblical heroes and villains, this particular apostle is one that Christian leaders can identify with the most. After all, he embodied many qualities of effective leaders: Drive to lead, courage to speak, risk-taking behavior. But he struggled with a few idols that continued to take hold of him throughout his life, namely pride, fear of people, and comfort, all of which led to the sin that shook him to the core of his being, namely denying Jesus.

It was pride, the mother of all sins, that propelled Peter to declare to Jesus and the other disciples the night before Jesus was arrested that his faith was unshakeable, 'Even if I must die with you, I will not deny you!' (Matthew 26:35). But the next morning, his imagination of boldly standing next to Jesus, defending him before the Sanhedrin, was completely shattered. Peter, who was supposed to be the rock, crumbled into pieces. Pride indeed comes before the fall.

The second idol, fear of people, had also been operational quite visibly throughout Peter's life and reared its ugly head when

Peter denied knowing his Lord in response to a non-threatening question by a teenage servant girl at the courtyard of the high priest. He gave in to cowardice and betrayal in order to gain acceptance and safety despite having been warned that he would deny Jesus. As such, he allowed fear of people's opinion to set the limit to his obedience.

Comfort was also prominent in Peter's life. When Jesus restored him following his denial, recommissioned him, and told him about his future martyrdom, Peter replied by asking what would happen with John. He was comparing his fate to his comrade, most possibly not out of brotherly concern, but the fear of missing out what John might have experienced that he would not. It was this desire for comfort that must have contributed to his denial in the first place. Though he had left his comfort zone to follow Jesus for three years, the prospect of suffering by his association with Jesus was too much to bear at the time.

In short, pride, fear of people, and comfort were the functional masters of Peter's heart that led to his denial of his true master. Together they created a powerful synergy to test and crush Peter's faith. Fear of people is an indicator of pride because it deludes us into thinking that we are responsible for our comfort and safety that only God can secure and maintain for us. When Peter was filled with fear of people's displeasure, he was playing god, arrogantly acting as if he was the person in charge of his own comfort and safety.

Similarly, in a stroke of genius that captures the psychological inner working of people's hearts, Powlison (2003, p. 153) gave a contemporary example of a prevailing sin might be triggered from diverse idols.

> For example, sexual immorality might occur for many different reasons: erotic pleasure, financial advantage, revenge on a spouse or parent, fear of saying no to an authority, pursuit of approval, enjoyment of power over another's sexual response, the quest for social status or career advancement, pity for someone and playing the savior, fear of losing a potential marriage partner, escape from boredom, peer pressure, and so forth. Wise biblical counselors dig for specifics. They don't

assume all people have the same characteristic flesh, or that a person always does a certain thing for the same reasons. The flesh is creative in iniquity.

The gospel and idolatrous desires

Thus far we have seen how idolatrous desires hold Christian leaders captive such that their leadership decisions and actions are bent out of shape. They will lose their saltiness in the world if they are being deceived by their own inordinate desire for power, approval, comfort, control, superiority, and independence. Being aware of these schemes of the "Devil" is a prerequisite to the ability to stand firm against them. But that's only half of the battle plan. In order to fight these idolatrous desires, they have to have a new desire that is more beautiful and captivating. They need the gospel of Jesus Christ.

As mentioned in the previous chapter, the word 'gospel' comes from the Greek word *euangelion*, which means good news. The gospel is historically understood as the good news that by God's unmerited grace, guilty sinners who deserve his just punishment have been fully pardoned and accepted on the grounds of the death and resurrection of Jesus Christ. The gospel tells us that we have been saved from God, by God, and for God alone.

We are saved from God's wrath

As image bearers of the Creator God, all people become sinful by nature and in rebellion against God, and are therefore subject to his holy and just wrath. It is a dreadful thing to fall into the hands of a holy and just God who is wrathful.

We are saved by God's sacrifice

God took the initiative to send Jesus Christ, His one and only Son, to the world to live the life we should have lived and die the death we deserve. Since the wrath of God was poured out on and fully satisfied in Jesus, all who believe in Christ Jesus are forever rescued from the penalty of sin.

We are saved for God's glory

God saved sinners through the death and resurrection of Christ for himself. We are recipients, but not the ultimate goal, of salvation. The grand story of salvation is the story of God's renewing all creation, restoring the broken world. And as his redeemed people, we now live and work for his glory, advancing his kingdom, redeeming all things towards the new heaven and earth.

Our short life on this side of heaven will never be long enough to plumb the depths of this gospel truth. We often fail to see the beauty of the gospel, hence it does not capture the imaginations of our hearts. The crisis of Christian leadership is due to this lack of savoring the gospel.

Christian leaders find it hard to relate the gospel to their leadership roles (e.g., the way they use power, how they relate to their staff, how they deal with criticism or handle conflicts, etc.). They assume that they know the gospel, but it often remains as head knowledge that does not have any bearing on their daily practices. My experiences training Christian leaders both in the church and the corporate contexts suggest that this knowing-doing gap is quite pervasive.

The gospel and Christian leaders

In this section I would suggest four salient features of the gospel and their relevance to Christian leaders. In other words, the nature and implications of the gospel are fleshed out in more details relative to their practical application to leaders.

1.   The gospel is the sine qua non of Christian leadership

Not only is it relevant to every Christian, it is absolutely essential for Christian leaders. Many treat the gospel as something that should be shared with unbelievers and taught to baby believers. It is the milk, not the meat of the Christian faith. The truth is, the gospel to the Christian faith is simultaneously the milk, the meat, the appetizer, the dessert, and the coffee and mint after the dessert!

We always need to drink from the bottomless well of the gospel regardless of whether we have been Christians for three minutes, three years, or three decades. To put it differently, the gospel is not just a starting point, it is *the* reference point for all leadership endeavors. A cursory reading of the New Testament shows that Paul always links many of the subjects he wrote in his letters to the gospel.

For example, Paul wrote to the saints in Ephesus about the grace-alone-through-faith-alone-in-Christ-alone gospel in the first three chapters of his letter, followed by practical application of that gospel in the three remaining chapters.

That is, Christian leaders should treat others (e.g., clients or colleagues) with kindness and tenderness without regard of their past mistakes because that is how they were treated by God in Christ. Their relationship with their boss must be characterized by an attitude of voluntary subordination as bondservants of Christ rather than people-pleasers.

On the flip side, unlike the cruel masters of the 1st century, they should be fair and considerate towards their staff, because they have received much more than what they deserve from God. Even the leaders' relationship at home with their spouse should also reflect that between Christ and his church, submitting to one another out of deference for Christ. In every case, Paul went to great lengths to show that the gospel should relate to every single dimension of our lives.

2. The sequence of the gospel

The gospel has a definite sequence of declaration and obligation. We need to understand that God does not grade us on a bell curve, plotting people based on their intensity in obeying his laws (or lack of it). Those who want to be justified based on their law-keeping should meet God's standard of absolute perfection. Since no humans can exemplify an utterly sinless life in obedience to God, the only way to be justified before God is through the righteousness of Christ, the perfect sinless one who died for our sins, imputed to us.

We are instantly declared righteous in Christ without any law-keeping or moral achievements, then and only then we are truly moved to live in joyful obedience in Christ. In other words, it follows the sequence of guilt-grace-gratitude – we are guilty of our sins, we are undeserved recipients of grace, we obey out of heartfelt gratitude.

When God rescued the Israelites from Egypt, he did not subject them to the ten commandments test prior to selecting who would pass it with flying colors. The ten commandments were given after they had their freedom from slavery. In fact, the first promise of the gospel in the book of Genesis was given without any terms and conditions outlining how we in our fallen state would react in response.

We should stop projecting ourselves as David who had to fight the Goliaths of our lives with bigger faith and valiant efforts. Because we are the Israelites who enjoyed the victory over the Goliath-sized life problems because Jesus Christ, the true and better David, has fought the ultimate battle for us and transferred his victory to us. Only then we can do things through him whose victory-securing strength continues to strengthen us.

This pattern of gospel declaration-obligation is even more pronounced and discernible in the New Testament, particularly in the Pauline letters. What we have to do is always predicated upon what Christ has done.

The implication of this truth on leadership identity is vital. God's grace is *not* dispensed to us commensurate with our ability to meet God's key performance indicators for corporate leaders (e.g., do not cheat on taxes, do not be greedy with profits, treat your staff well, care for the environment). That would constitute the opposite sequence, obligation-declaration, a moralistic pattern that will see us living our lives in quiet desperation, grappling with guilt and fear on the treadmill of performance, perpetually wondering whether we have done enough to earn his approval and blessings.

On the contrary, the declaration-obligation pattern suggests that we still obey God's laws, not out of fear but out of gratitude knowing that we have been the recipient of God's unmerited grace in Christ despite our imperfect performance. When performance becomes the foundation of leaders' identity, the idols of power and control will usurp the throne of their hearts. We will discuss more in-depth how the gospel radically changes leaders' identity and dignity in the next two chapters.

3. The sufficiency of the gospel

God's ultimate blessings are found in the gospel. He did not give us in instalments. His divine power has given us everything we need in Christ Jesus for a godly life (2 Peter 1:3), and that includes godly leadership. The extent to which we find Christ is enough for us will determine our capacity to lead effectively, without needing the adoration, attention, or affection of people, for they are merely our fellow sinners who will disappoint us. While those legitimate things are wonderful to be enjoyed as blessings from God, they are dreadful to be worshipped as rulers.

Since the gospel, the fountain of living water that gives and continues giving, it is foolish to keep trying to dig the cracked cisterns that give only polluted water. The gospel guards leaders from the tendency to live for people's approval or in pursuit of power. Note that even Jesus' inner circles were not immune from them. James and John were blinded by power, and Peter was crippled by fear of people.

4. The nature of the gospel

The gospel does not express, contain, or result in the power of God. It *is* the power of God (Romans 1:16). It is the power of God that saves us from idols, sin, death, hell, and ourselves. No doubt the gospel is the greatest thing since sliced bread (even light years before sliced bread was even invented!).

But by nature it is offensive and scandalous to human minds because it is designed to please God and him alone. Small wonder therefore efforts to pervert, dilute, or modify the Gospel have persisted for ages.

The gospel offends our *pride*. It tells us that we cannot save us from ourselves, we therefore need a Savior. Living in our fallen nature in the fallen world, we are not only part of the cosmic problem, we are the core problem. The gospel therefore gives no credit at all to us in the design, process, and outcome for salvation; it is all the work of the Triune God for us.

The gospel also offends our *wisdom* because it saves us through something many consider as utter foolishness, i.e., God becoming man and dying a humiliating, disgraceful death on our behalf. We are supposed to believe in something that goes against scientific knowledge and personal experience, i.e., Jesus Christ rose from the dead in a glorious new body, and he would never die again. Without a divine revelation, and illumination for us to understand that revelation, it is impossible to believe in what otherwise sounds like an outlandish concoction of a cosmic salvation project.

Because the gospel shows us that we have zero contributions to the solution of our biggest problem, it will keep our ego in check. Many leaders are aware that pride comes before destruction, but they still fall from grace in the end because of the extremely lethal, gradual, shapeshifting manner with which pride operates in their lives. To continually remind ourselves that we are merely sinners saved by grace will protect them from the sense of entitlements that typically creeps up on leaders.

References

Augustine, S., & Watts, W. (1979). *Saint Augustine's confessions.* Cambridge, MA: Harvard University Press.

Beale, G. K. L. (2008). *We become what we worship: A biblical theology of idolatry.* Nottingham, England: IVP Academic.

Blanken, I., van de Nen, N., & Zeelenberg, M. (2015). A meta-analytic review of moral licensing. *Personality and Social Psychology Bulletin*, 41(4), 540–558.

Bryce, R. (2003). *Pipe dreams: Greed, ego, and the death of Enron.* New York: Public Affairs.

Brueggemann, W. (1998). *A commentary on Jeremiah.* Grand Rapids, MI: Eerdmans.

Cruver, B. (2003). *Enron: Anatomy of greed* (p. 10). London: Arrow Books.

Fusaro, P. C., & Miller, R. M. (2002). *What went wrong at Enron.* Hoboken: John Wiley.

Graham, D. A. (2019). *The unchecked corruption of Trump's cabinet.* www.theatlantic.com/ideas/archive/2019/05/watchdog-ben-carsons-table-spending-broke-law/589804/. Accessed July 3, 2019.

Hofmann, W., Kotabe, H. P., Vohs, K. D., & Baumeister, R. F. (2015). Desire and desire regulation. In W. Hofmann & L. F. Nordgren (Eds.), *The psychology of desire* (pp. 61–81). New York, NY, US: The Guilford Press.

Keller, T. (2008). *The reason for God: Belief in an age of skepticism.* New York: Dutton.

Keller, T. (2009). *Counterfeit gods: The empty promises of money, sex, and power, and the only hope that matters.* New York: Dutton.

Kirkpatrick, S. A., & Locke, E. (1991). Leadership: Do traits matter? *The Executive*, 5(2), 48–60.

Lewis, C.S. (1968). *Mere Christianity.* San Francisco: Harper Collins.

Mazar, N., & Zhong, C. B. (2010). Do green products make us better people? *Psychological Science*, 21, 494–498.

Merritt, A. C., Effron, D. A., & Monin, B. (2010). Moral self-licensing: When being good frees us to be bad. *Social and Personality Psychology Compass*, 4, 344–357.

Powlison, D. (1995). Idols of the heart and "vanity fair". *Journal of Biblical Counseling*, 13(2), 35–50.

Powlison, D. (2003). *Seeing with new eyes: Counseling and the human condition through the lens of scripture.* Phillipsburg, NJ: P&R Publishing.

Smith, J. K. A. (2009). *Desiring the kingdom: Worship, worldview and cultural formation.* Grand Rapids, MI: Baker Academic.

CHAPTER 3

How the gospel creates leading servants

'If serving is below you, leading is beyond you'
(Anonymous)

In a good leadership textbook, typically you will find nested within the discussion of leadership the definition of what is classically called the 'Hitler problem' of leadership. The central question would revolve around whether or not Hitler was actually a leader. Based on his perceived influence over Germany in particular, it is assumed that Adolf Hitler must be seen as a leader despite the ensuing negative leadership effects on followers (for fuller discussion, see Sendjaya, 2005).

However, to consider Hitler a leader is to commit a serious theoretical blunder. Proponents of moral-laden leadership theories aptly remarked that 'under morally attractive theories, Hitler is not a leader at all. He is a bully or tyrant or simply the head of Germany.' (Ciulla, 1995, p. 13). In a similar vein, a president or prime minister might be a mere head of state or government, but not a leader in the real sense of the word.

The above example highlights the single greatest error in the understanding of leadership that is shared by both practitioners and, to a certain extent, scholars. That is, the tendency to treat as synonymous 'the leader' and 'the person occupying a position in the organizational hierarchy'.

One might be a director, manager, supervisor, chair, pastor, or minister, but that individual may not necessarily be a leader. They are merely role occupants or position holders if their decisions and actions unmistakably suggest the absence of real leadership despite the authority they possess.

On the flip side, there are countless individuals who do not occupy positional power yet exemplify impactful acts of leadership (e.g., one might think of individuals like Mother Teresa or Mahatma Gandhi). It is therefore more useful both in academic research and everyday practice/conversation to decouple 'leadership' from 'organizational positions'. Everyone can play a leadership role despite the lack of formal positions of authority.

Once we remove this fallacy away from our leadership parlance, we can start thinking of leadership in a much more accurate and nuanced manner. That is, rather than treating leadership as a trait-like property that individuals have as soon as they occupy a position, it is more accurate to consider it a state-like quality that individuals might take on and off at different times in their position.

In other words, rather than merely saying 'X is a leader', we should ask how 'X is leader-like or a real leader' in a specific context. This distinction is important because even the most seasoned leaders can at times act in ways that do not exemplify leadership (e.g., failing to confront someone who bullies others for fear of retaliation). Having this accurate perspective will help us appreciate the importance of leaders' personal identity.

Leaders' self-identity

All major theories in the leadership field (e.g., trait theories, leader-member exchange transformational, authentic) emphasize the importance of understanding how leaders see and define themselves, and how these self-identities develop, change, and are influenced by leader-follower interactions. An accurate understanding of leaders' self-identity provides key insights into why leaders behave the way they do.

Academic work in the field of self-identity was largely initiated by the works of philosopher William James in the late 18th century, and continues to flourish as a key construct in social psychology. In its evolution, the locus of the study moved from a preoccupation with the individual to the social understanding of the relational self and collective self. That is, one's identity is often formed not only from one's personal idiosyncratic attributes such as physical features (e.g., I am tall), psychological traits (e.g., I am an introvert), abilities (e.g., I analyze big data), or interests (e.g., I love reading poetry) but also from salient group characteristics.

In other words, who we are is a function of our similarities and differences with others. This social identification is essentially a perception of oneness with or belongingness to some human categories.

Consider for illustration purposes Alexandra, an advertising agency executive. She may define herself in terms of the group(s) with which she identifies herself (e.g., I am an Australian; I am a woman; I am highly educated; I am successful). She perceives herself as an actual or symbolic member of the group(s) and based on that association with the group would perceive the fate of the group(s) as her own.

Self-identity may be ascribed (i.e., involuntary and inherently deep-rooted) or non-ascribed (i.e., chosen or voluntary). Although Alexandra can choose to adopt the (non-ascribed) identity of an executive, her (ascribed) identity as a female is inherited.

Research suggests that we construct identities based on the appropriate contexts to give meaning and direction to our activities (Ashforth & Schinoff, 2016; Hannah, Woolfolk, & Lord, 2009). To continue the example, Alexandra manages five people in her team and reports to the marketing director. When she chairs the Monday morning meetings with her direct reports, she would have self-schemas of 'leadership' activated and hence her identity as a leader is salient. Characteristics such as authoritative, bold, strategic, and considerate are manifested when she interacts with them in the meeting.

On the other hand, when she has to give the weekly report to the marketing director, her identity as 'follower' is more salient in that context. As such, she would exemplify other characteristics such as proactive, competent, industrious, and attentive.

The above dynamic shows that identity construction is a situated, embodied, and rational process. This context-specific self-identity incorporates multiple active factors such as one's organizational role, one's superior or subordinate, and one's work task. As such, we always face two questions at any given time: 'Who am I in this situation?' and 'what should I do?' Once a specific self-schema is activated in a specific social context, it will subconsciously regulate our behavior (Brown & Smart, 1991)

In this chapter I will delimit our discussion to non-ascribed leadership role identities that one adopts, with a particular focus on being a 'leader' or 'servant'. No doubt we may embody other role-related selves in other contexts (e.g., being a parent or a spouse at home, which might be less salient as a behavioral guide at work).

This difference in the extent to which people self-define as 'leaders' or 'servants' is a crucial point of distinction. Some leaders self-define themselves more strongly as 'leaders'; others self-define themselves more strongly as 'servants'. Within the work context, some leadership role occupants might see the 'self as leader' identity as something central to their self-conception whilst others see it as a peripheral self-conception.

Research confirms that relative to peripheral self-conceptions, central self-conceptions are stronger predictors of the way we interact with others (Markus & Wurf, 1987). For example, those who view themselves more as leaders will have more readiness to make important decisions on behalf of others, or take a new initiative without consulting others.

Why is this an important issue to consider? Because the leader self-definition serves as a meta-structure guiding the way they relate to others. Many leaders feel ambivalent about how they should see themselves in the continuum between leaders and servants, particularly Christian leaders who realize that they are simultaneously leaders and servants.

Should they primarily see themselves as leaders who serve or servants who lead? The difference between their central self-definition as 'leaders' or 'servants' will manifest in observable behaviors. The ensuing paragraphs will delineate further the notion and formation of personal identity.

Personal identity: A leader or a servant?

Personal identity is a complex subject because our personal identity cannot be separated from the social context we find ourselves in. As we are influencing and being influenced by others, our personal identity can be very straightforward or ambiguous. While we can clearly say with confidence that a person is or is not a male, it is much more complex to identify whether a person is or is not a 'good Christian'. That is because while gender comprises one attribute, being a 'good Christian' may include multiple attributes (e.g., pray and read the Bible on a regular basis, serving in a local church or community, growing in faith). In fact, we can have a heated discussion for hours to establish the criteria by which to decide the relative importance of each attribute.

In a similar vein, having the identity of a 'leader' or 'servant' can be ambiguous as each includes multiple distinct attributes. A good 'leader' might be expected to cast a vision, mobilize people to march towards the same drumbeat, etc. On the other hand, a good 'servant' could be one who prioritizes other people's needs, willingly employs personal resources to help others, etc.

While many Christians would agree that these attributes of leadership and servanthood can be found in the bible, it is rather tricky to arrive at a consensus on their relative importance. The ambiguity is exacerbated by the fact that these attributes or behaviors are not only biblically based, but also socially constructed and contextually bound.

For example, what should or should not be done by a leader or a servant in the West might be different from that in the East. At the risk of stereotyping, leaders in the East are typically expected to be authoritative and benevolent, acting as a patriarch or matriarch who treats their staff as members of their own family. In other words, they have to be paternalistic in their leadership approach. This paternalistic leadership approach fits the highly collectivistic contexts but might be difficult to implement in highly individualistic contexts (e.g., United States, Australia). In other words, the extent to which one can enact behaviors that are aligned with the social expectations of the local culture determines one's effort to internalize one's self-definition as 'leader' or 'servant'.

Internalizing personal identity

Individuals explore their identity as a 'leader' based on the assumptions they develop over time through personal experience (e.g., with family, church, school), observations (e.g., of role models), and exposures (e.g., to books, media). From this natural conflation of influences, they form a schema for what a leader looks like in terms of attributes, behaviors, and skills.

To illustrate, let's consider Joe, a twenty-something year old theological seminary graduate who is about to have a placement in a congregation. Joe has some idea of what sort of church leader he wants to be. He might have a schema of leadership that is oriented towards paternalistic-authoritarian ('a pastor should emphasize the truth') or humble servants ('a pastor should have a readiness to serve').

Out of multiple possible schemas of leadership that he has developed awareness of throughout his life and seminary training, he experiments with one of them and engages in an *internal-to-self* comparison process. To put it differently, he chooses to implement a schema on the basis of his understanding of what makes an effective church leader.

To keep things simple, let's assume that he considers two alternatives. He might choose to apply the humble servant approach because Jesus was a meek and gentle leader towards the needy people around him. The second option is the paternalistic-authoritarian approach because Jesus was very firm and bold towards the self-righteous people. Trying on this schema on a provisional basis, Joe then takes small steps to act like a leader to test the water.

What Joe is involved in is a process called 'identity work', a process of identity formation in which individuals engage in to create, repair, maintain, strengthen, or revise the construction of self-concept (Sveningsson & Alvesson, 2003). Every emerging leader would actively engage in identity work despite the fact the 'leader' identity might be readily assumed in the formal organizational hierarchy or emerge in response to a calling, crisis, or training.

Underlying this notion of identity experimentation is an interpersonal process of claiming by the self and granting by others (Bartel & Dutton, 2001; DeRue & Ashford, 2010). When individuals show specific verbal or non-verbal behaviors to assert certain characteristics that are essential to a particular personal identity, they engage in claiming acts. Granting acts are verbal and non-verbal behaviors that others in a social interaction signal whether or not they assert the person's identity.

Here are examples of claiming acts that Joe might choose to perform. He asserts his identity as a leader in the congregation by ensuring that his language and appearance project the image of a pastor (e.g., no more colloquial language, or ribbed and faded jeans!). He would announce his office hours and encourage the congregation to make appointments to see him for consultation. In meetings, Joe often highlights his expertise in the Christian doctrines and by extension his wisdom in solving an issue. He always takes the seat at the head of a meeting table in every meeting and often makes the decision on behalf of the other church leaders. While Joe certainly has a desire to express his assumed leader personal identity, he is not entirely sure at this stage whether other people also see him as a leader.

On the flip side, a granting act by others towards Joe occurs when the lay leaders in the church leadership team defer to Joe's preference for important decisions. That granting act serves as an affirmation for Joe that he has the qualities expected of a pastor. Conversely, if decisions seem to be made by a few senior and influential lay leaders without an expressed request for Joe's opinion or feedback, this gesture might signal disaffirmation of his leadership.

Note that while the church has collectively confirmed that Joe is hired as their pastor, thus implying a formal role in the church structure, as aforementioned this role-granting act may not necessarily imply a 'granting' of leadership. The jury is still out. The lay leaders of the church are yet to grant Joe a leader identity, and they would do so only if they see a match between their individual and collective schemas of leadership and Joe's attributes and skills (cf. Lord & Maher, 1991).

If they perceive that Joe acts in ways that are incompatible with their existing schemas of leadership, they might not grant Joe a leader identity. For example, they expect Joe to be visionary and bold in enacting strategic changes within the church, but it turns out that his concern lies in the maintenance of ongoing church programs.

The social dynamic in the mutual claiming and granting behaviors is key in the process of internalizing a multifaceted personal identity such as a leader. Personal identity internalization is not so much a formal, cognitive process as a social, instinctive process where verbal and non-verbal acts are enacted to affirm or disaffirm the identity in question.

The 'powerful leader' identity

Following the discussion of the theoretical underpinning of identity formation, we will now turn to the practical application of how this plays out in Christian leaders. I would submit that an overwhelming majority of Christian leaders would be more likely to internalize a personal identity as 'leader' relative to 'servant' (i.e., those who would be more likely to say to themselves, 'I am their leader', as opposed to 'I am their servant'). While there are Christian leaders who might be more attuned to the ideal of servanthood (which we will discuss later), the number is comparatively smaller than those who aspire to be a strong and powerful leader.

The rationale is quite simple. People in leadership positions by definition are endowed with power. There is an intricate and natural link between leadership and power. While powerful individuals are not necessarily leaders, leadership always implies possession of power. Being in a leadership position affords an individual the power to make decisions that will affect other individuals or the entire organization.

The higher one moves in the organizational hierarchy, the bigger the power one commands and the magnitude of the decisions (as an extreme example, think about President Harry Truman's decision to drop the atomic bomb on the city of Hiroshima in 1945). When one has arrived after years of climbing the corporate ladder at a top position in the hierarchy, his or her self-definition as leader has typically become a central part of their self-concept.

As leaders claim and internalize the 'powerful leader' identity, the ensuing sense of exhilaration can subtly trigger an unhealthy dose of narcissism or excessive self-love (Kets de Vries, 1993). That is because increased power implies increased distance from subordinates, leading to self-perception of superiority and pride. When that happens, there is an erosion of the inherent value of power within the leader. The erosion process often occurs in such a gradual process that the power holders fail to recognize its emergence and effects on themselves. Many leaders treat power initially as something to share with others; however it soon becomes something they anxiously hoard and reserve for themselves.

It is worth noting that it is not always power that corrupts. Clinical psychology research repeatedly confirms that the roots of abusive power are often found in men and women who were once victimized by power. While Lord Acton's oft-quoted maxim that 'Power tends to corrupt and absolute power corrupts absolutely' still haunts many leaders today, the exact opposite phenomenon is also equally pervasive. Edgar Friedenberg once wrote a more sobering rationale why power corrupts, 'All weakness tends to corrupt and impotence corrupts absolutely.' It is powerlessness, whether perceived or real, that often propels people to attain and wield power in destructive ways. When victims become perpetrators, the damage caused is escalated to a much greater proportion.

The issue therefore is not *how much* power leaders should have, but *why* they want to obtain power in the first place. History is riddled with cases of leaders preoccupied with power. They went to great lengths to obtain it and guard it at all costs. Such leaders first manage their power, then before long their power manages them. It will be wise for Christian leaders to remember that 'power is a powerful narcotic – animating, life-sustaining, addictive. The people who have it generally have worked hard to obtain it and are not overkeen to let it go' (Kets De Vries, 1993, p. 38).

This tendency has been around since the dawn of human civilization. Even the disciples of Jesus were arguing about who was the greatest among them (cf. Mark 9:33–37), and that heated argument occurred immediately after Jesus told them that he was going to be captured and killed. Jesus sat them down and clarified what their request really meant. However, their lust for power must have been deeply embedded within their hearts for they repeated the same request in such a short time (cf. Mark 10:35–45). James and John asked if they can occupy preeminent positions at the right and left hand of Jesus when he reigns in glory. The fact that the remaining disciples were indignant at the Zebedee brothers upon hearing their request showed that the fear of missing out on positions of power was pervasive among them.

For the umpteenth time, Jesus explained that leadership is about service, not power. 'Whoever *wants* to become great among you *must* be your servant, and whoever *wants* to be first *must* be slave of all' (Mark 10:43–44, NIV). Implicit in that exhortation is our fixation on power; hence we tend to lean towards the 'want' side of the equation and ignore the 'must' side. We want greatness, influence, authority, and we seek to attain them with as little service and sacrifice as possible. We want the crown without the cross, glory without suffering. We want to be masters without becoming servants. We use our roles, responsibilities, and platforms as stepping stones to occupy the seats of honor next to Jesus.

The same dynamic occurs within power-hungry megachurch pastors who fall from grace. Given their chosen central self-definition as 'the leader', they would engage in overt claiming acts to ensure people fully acknowledge and accept their leadership. A particular former megachurch senior pastor who shall remain nameless is a case in point. Having planted a church and led it to exponential growth, he engaged in identity-claiming acts by proposing to change the church bylaws to afford him increased decision-making power. Despite major concerns raised by other leaders in the church, he proceeded with the idea and rewrote the bylaws.

His desire for increased decision-making power is fueled by his growing sense of entitlement. While power can raise both a sense of entitlement and responsibility on the power holder (Tjosvold & van Knippenberg, 2009), often it is the sense of entitlement that emerges more strongly. There are two types of entitlements one might develop: (1) merit-based entitlements, which are given commensurate with one's abilities, efforts, and/or achievements, and (2) psychological entitlements, which are based on perceptions that one deserves preferential treatment, notwithstanding one's actual abilities, effort levels, or other justification (Campbell, Bonacci, Shelton, Exline, & Bushman, 2004).

In the case of this senior pastor above, while it is true that his capacity, achievements, and hard work were exemplary, he increasingly felt that the astronomical growth of the church should be attributed solely to him. He claimed that the most important brand to develop was not the church, but himself. His was a growing sense of psychological entitlement (Harvey & Martinko, 2009).

After a few major turns of events, a public letter signed by nine other pastors of the church demanded him to step down from all aspects of ministry and leadership. The letter specifically isolated abuse of power as the main character flaw, citing his domineering spirit, arrogance, quick temper, and harsh speech. The nine pastors subsequently left the church. What followed was a detailed investigation launched by the Board of Overseers involving more than a thousand hours of research that resulted in a 200-page document. The saga ended with a sudden, voluntary resignation of the senior pastor.

There is no doubt that Christian leaders have a high calling of overseeing others without being overbearing on others. They cannot act as if the whole counsel of God resides in them and demand that people trust and obey them no matter what. Note that these leaders do not necessarily do bad things. They are doing good things, and doing them with all their might. However, in the process, they treat people merely as pawns in their grand agenda. They become domineering taskmasters who demand from their followers much more than their God-given capacity to give. When they see followers as a means to an end, they would typically employ manipulation and coercion tactics.

In order to justify the manner with which they treat their staff, they might argue that it is done because we are serving an excellent God who demands excellence from us. Granted there is nothing wrong with that. Excellence is a thoroughly biblical virtue. But what often happens is excellence becomes a façade to cover the leader's blind ambition. As such, excellence is turned from a good and biblical virtue into an ultimate and idolatrous virtue.

Christian leaders only fool themselves if they choose to ignore the fact that they are infallible human beings. They are prone to wander. They are prone to leave the God they serve. Regardless of how much success they have had in God's works, they are merely sinners saved by grace and in need of that grace every day. They are not, and will never be, sinner emeritus. When it comes to the grace of God, Christian leaders are as needy as the people they lead.

Pride and power

In order to understand our fixation with power, we need to consider something more fundamental that dwells within our hearts, namely our pride. It is an old-age wisdom that is both timeless and timely, 'Pride goes before destruction and haughty spirit before a fall' (Proverbs 16:18).

You have probably heard a simile that says pride in many ways is like bad breath, everyone except ourselves knows we have it. But the comparison ends there, for pride is much more serious than bad breath. It is more akin to a highly contagious disease.

If we catch it, we do not feel anything, yet other people around us feel nauseous and suffer tremendously. It affects everyone without prejudice, rich or poor, evil or good, atheist or theist, Conservative or Liberal, Arminian or Calvinist.

Interestingly, the highest infection rate is often found among the population of leaders relative to the general population. The more power the leaders have, the more malignant the disease is. It spreads faster within their mind, emotion, and will, and to other humans through direct and indirect contact. For thousands of years, efforts to eradicate this disease have largely failed.

Tracing the origin of this communicable disease has led to the identification of its first carriers (i.e., patient zero), namely Adam and Eve. After being banned from the Garden of Eden because of their rebellion to God, they transmitted to their descendants a hidden virus that goes into latency deep within the human nervous system.

Obtaining power has been singled out as a critical trigger that wakes up this virus from its deep slumber. One of Abraham Lincoln's biographers wrote, 'If you want to find out what a man is to the bottom, give him power. Any man can stand adversity – only a great man can stand prosperity' (Alger, 1883).

A case in point is King Uzziah. In the book of Second Chronicles, we read that he was only sixteen years of age when he began his reign as a king. He began well, doing what was right in the eyes of the Lord, and God made him a successful king (2 Chronicles 26:4). His name was revered among other foreign nations including the Philistines, the Arabians, the Meunites, and the Ammonites. His fame spread afar for he was marvellously helped by God himself (2 Chronicles 26:15). That was the climax of his leadership, for things started to go south from that point onwards. The sleeping virus of pride was activated. 'But when he was strong, he grew proud, to his destruction' (2 Chronicles 26:16).

Many leadership authors claim 'success breeds success', but what often happens with leaders is the opposite, 'success breeds failure'. That is because power, influence, and status are notoriously known as catalysts of pride. Uzziah was under the delusion that it was he who made things happen. He had a sudden amnesia, forgetting the fact that it is the Lord his God that gave him the power to experience victory after victory. He began well, but finished miserably. He was struck with leprosy to the day of his death, and his leadership was relegated to a footnote in history as a classic cautionary tale of arrogance.

In contemporary organizations, we have numerous examples of highly successful executives who demonstrate excessive self-confidence. Their leadership success is typically attributed to their admirable leadership qualities. They are highly focused, result-driven, and intensely competitive. However, these same qualities can also lead to a leader's downfall. A leader's strengths and weaknesses are like two sides of the same coin. Leaders with strong conviction often think they are always right and do not need inputs from others. Many executives ignore that at their own peril.

Today this leadership hubris manifests in their engagement with public on social media. Using the social media platform to build their personal brand and with millions of fans ready to defend them at any cost, they would tweet words that merely reflect nothing but streams of consciousness. They also tweet offensive comments and baseless accusations just because they feel entitled to.

Left unchecked, over-confidence in one's self and over-reliance on one's way of doing things can quickly change an otherwise effective leader into a destructive one. For every great product or company that these highly confident leaders build, there are countless employees who increasingly feel their feedback and complaints are completely ignored and thus become demoralized. Research on executive hubris repeatedly shows that intentional efforts need to be done to mitigate its negative effects on leadership effectiveness.

They should surround themselves with trusted, mature, and independent followers who are given permission to ask difficult questions around the leaders' vulnerable areas. Strong leaders in particular need a constant reminder that they are neither infallible nor indispensable. While competence might take them to the top, it is humility that keeps them there.

The insights on pride from C.S. Lewis (1952) is instructive. He wrote a three-pronged rationale why pride is a cardinal sin, more heinous than other typical leadership sins such as anger and greed: (1) the devil became the devil by pride, (2) pride is the cause of every other sin, and (3) pride is the total anti-God (and anti-others) state of mind.

We often think that one becomes arrogant because he is rich, smart, successful, or powerful. But what actually makes us arrogant is the perceived superiority we have vis-à-vis other people that matter to us. Our pride rears its ugly head when we think we are more powerful or successful than others. If others have an equal number of successes or power, we have no cause for arrogance. As such, pride satisfies itself not knowing that we have something, but that we have something more than others.

The smugness of the Pharisee in Luke 18 aptly illustrates this point. He prayed, 'God, I thank you that I am not like other men, extortioners, unjust, adulterers, or even like this tax collector' (Luke 18:11). The Pharisee was full of himself, but always in comparison to others and to the tax collector near him. What we often do not notice with that prayer is that it was uttered in the deep recesses of his heart. No one heard the prayer except himself (and God, of course). Leaders beware: Pride is such an insidious sin, so difficult to detect and arduous to admit because it does not have to emerge to the surface as words, attitudes, or behaviors.

The more I read about pride from classic authors like C.S. Lewis, Andrew Murray, and Jeremy Taylor, the more I understand why they in unison assert that it is the subtlest sin of all. The proof of its subtlety is self-evident. By citing those classic authors on the subject of pride, I might be showing off my cognitive mastery of the subject. I might project the image that I am fully aware of the subtle effects of pride, and that I have learned to deal with pride and remain humble instead. That image of a humble leader would command people's respect and praise. When I secretly enjoy all that extra attention, the next thing I know is that I am basking in my humility!

That is why the first step in dealing with pride is, as Lewis rightly argues, to admit that we are the owners of proud hearts. I am not sure what the last step is, but I am pretty sure that is the first step. Ignore that, and we will deal with God himself, who actively opposed the proud (Proverbs 16:5; James 4:6; 1 Peter 5:5). Indeed, it is a terrifying thing to fall into the hands of the living God.

▮ The 'humble servant' identity

As aforementioned, the opposite of the 'powerful leader' identity is the 'humble servant' identity. If power fuels pride, and Christian leaders should be wary of claiming the 'powerful leader' identity, should they instead embrace the 'humble servant' identity? In order to answer that question, we should consider more in-depth the notion of servant in the Bible. I submit that there are at least four reasons that underlie why the idea that leaders should be servants are repulsive to many. These reasons are deeply embedded in our cognitive schema, shaping our gross misunderstanding of the intricate, rich, and complex nature of servanthood in the Bible.

First, a persistent neglect of the etymology of the word 'servant' in the New Testament is a key reason behind a total neglect of the idea of 'leader as servant'. Often overlooked is the richness of the biblical word picture behind the word 'servant', defined in most dictionaries as 'one that serves others'. 'Servant' as an identity is much more pervasive in the Bible relative to 'leader'. There are only six occurrences of the phrase 'leader' in the King James Bible, as those raised by God to lead were called 'servants'. When Moses in the Old Testament was called to lead the Israelites out of Egypt, he was not referred to by God as 'Moses, my leader', but 'Moses, my servant'.

Second, the New Testament employs seven Greeks words interchangeably to denote the word 'servant' in the English Bible (i.e., *diakonos, doulos, pais, sundoulos, oiketes, therapon,* and *huperetes,* cf.

Vine, 1985). Altogether these words occur over three hundred times in the New Testament. Each of these words has its own association with the cultural settings of the biblical times. A close scrutiny of these words using bible dictionaries and Greek lexicon indicates that the concept of 'servant' is pregnant with meaning, as the following paragraphs delineate.

The word *diakonos* literally means 'someone who waits at the table', referring to the person who renders service during a meal (Bennett, 1998) as depicted in Jesus' parable in the Gospel of Luke 17:8. Implicit in the usage of the word are lessons for disciples to wait at the table and serve others instead of sitting at the head-table and seeking to be served. The English word 'deacon' is derived from *diakonos*, which is commonly used to describe a leader in the context of a local church. Embedded within the use of the word *diakonos* is the emphasis on humility and selfless service. Hence, in Jesus' terms, leadership is not about power and personal aggrandizement, but about offering one's self in service to others.

Doulos is the most frequently used word for 'servant' in the New Testament both in the literal and figurative senses (Getz, 1984). Literally speaking, the word simply denotes the natural condition of those who live as slaves to their masters (Vine, 1985). However, contrary to the common understanding, the use of *doulos* in the Bible refers to the notion of subjection without the idea of bondage. The same emphasis is also found in the figurative use of the word *doulos* in the New Testament (Vine, 1985). The word *doulos* was frequently used metaphorically to describe positive spiritual, moral, and ethical conditions (i.e., in bondage of God) as well as negative connotations (i.e., in bondage of sin or corruption). On the whole, while the word *doulos* was often taken in its strongest sense to mean a slave who gives himself up to another's will in disregard of his own interests, it signifies a voluntary act of subordination performed in the context of Christian love for God and others. This voluntary subordination is manifested in the willingness to assume the lowliest of positions and endure hardship and suffering on behalf of other people.

The other words, while less frequently used, are significant to consider in efforts to have a holistic understanding of servant. *Pais* signifies an attendant, particularly the king's attendant (Vine,

1985). *Sundoulos* means fellow servant, which corresponds to the notion of an associate or colleague who is subject to the same authority (Thayer, 1996). *Oiketes* refers to a household servant who lives in the same house as the householder (Locyker, 1986). *Therapon* denotes an attendant or servant of God and spoken with dignity of Moses who faithfully carried out the duties assigned to him by God (Thayer, 1996). Finally, *huperetes* literally means an under-rower or subordinate rower, which signifies 'those who row in the lower tier of a trireme (an ancient Greek three-tiered warship), and then came to mean those who do anything under another, and hence simply "underlings"' (Robertson & Plummer, 1914, p. 74). In the contemporary sense, it could well be translated as 'subordinate'.

Taken together, the seven Greek words for servant suggest a willingness and readiness to be subservient before others in obedient gratitude, so that others' needs and interests are served. None of these words insinuate a lack of self-respect or low self-image. While some words may indicate that the subordination is imposed on someone because of his or her lowly status, the humble position is voluntarily assumed and an act of service is wholeheartedly performed for the sake of others.

The third reason is perhaps most often overlooked, hence most important to understand. The servant identity has never been popular throughout the ages because of the unpleasant and embarrassing memory of slavery, particularly for those living in many parts of the English-speaking world. That is why the very notion of leaders as 'servants' is typically treated with contempt. This widespread attitude is unfortunate but understandable as it more often than not emerges from ignorance. Many Christian leaders do not want to consider themselves 'servants' because they conjure up images such as slavery, bondage, and other negative connotations from the Dark Ages.

A careful study of servanthood in the Bible reveals that there is a huge difference between the nature of slavery in the 1st century Greco-Roman world and 16th century New World. In the biblical era, people can opt to go into slavery because they have fallen into debt. They cannot declare bankruptcy because there was no law or government who can legally dissolve their debts. As such, they rely on creditors to pay the debt and are obligated to work for the creditor. Unlike the 16th century slavery, however, the creditors do not own the slaves, they merely owned the labor for a duration of time until the debt is fully paid.

In his fine work explicating the nature of slavery in the Bible by comparing Jewish, Greek, Roman, and ancient slavery in the 1st century BC, Harris (1999, p. 44) reached the following conclusion:

> In the first century, slaves were not distinguishable from free persons by race, by speech or by clothing; they were some-times more highly educated than their owners and held responsible professional positions; some persons sold themselves into slavery for economic or social advantage; they could reasonably hope to be emancipated after ten to twenty years of service or by thirties at the latest; they were not denied the right of public assembly and were not socially segregated (at least in the cities); they could accumulate savings to buy their freedom; their natural inferiority was not assumed.

It is estimated that during that the end of the 1st century BC in Italy, there were two million slaves out of a total population of six million. They worked in various occupations from farm laborers to city clerks, from cooks to shop managers, from cleaners to salaried executives of the state or a business (Harris, 1999).

Since the institution of slavery as part of a way of life, how-ever, no doubt there were malpractices and abuses that occurred. But broadly speaking it was in a stark contrast to the permanent, coercion-based, and morally reprehensible 16th century institution of slavery, which led to its abolition in the second half of the 18th century.

The fourth and final reason why the servant identity is typically shunned by Christian leaders is the failure to grasp the difference between the literal and metaphorical use of slavery, as they often appear in the New Testament in particular. Again Harris (1999) is instructive when he argues that the Christian teaching primarily focuses on the metaphorical or figurative language of slavery rather than literal or physical. Regarding the latter, following a comprehensive survey of extant literature, Harris (1999) concluded that Christianity did not endorse slavery as an absolute possession or inhuman use of one human being by another, yet at the same time the movement was not focused on social reform to abolish slavery as a social institution but on the transformation of character and conduct. While the biblical teaching of equality and freedom slowly led to the eventual destruction of physical slavery, the burden of the New Testament teaching rests on the metaphorical slavery to depict one's relation to God or Christ. Harris (1999, p. 86) summarizes it well as follows:

> So, then, in true Christian liberty, freedom *from* is immediately succeeded by freedom *for*. We are set free from slavery to sin precisely in order to be free to choose slavery to Christ, a slavery of perfect freedom . . . Such a transfer of allegiance, such an exchange of masters, saves us from falling prey to the danger of using liberty as an opportunity or pretext for evil and the danger of becoming liberty's slave.

The apostle Paul modelled this act of upside-down leadership when he wrote to the Corinthians, 'Though I am free and belong to no one, I have made myself a slave to everyone, to win as many as possible' (1 Corinthians 9:19, NIV Bible). Inspired partly by this verse, church father Martin Luther (1943, p. 5) penned the following words (as this is written in the 1940s, do not let its gender-specific language deter from its meaning): 'A Christian man is a perfectly free lord of all, subject to none. A Christian man is a perfectly dutiful servant of all, subject to all.' Applied to Christian leadership, it essentially means that in relation to their liberating God, leaders are subject to nobody with respect to liberty, yet they are subject to everyone with respect to service.

In sum, the association between the 'humble servant' as a leadership identity and the 16th century slavery stems from an ignorance of historical facts. It will be a remiss to jettison altogether the 'humble servant' identity on the basis of an unfounded fear that its practice will see the proliferation of modern-day slavery. Indeed, it will be a classic case of throwing the baby with the bathwater. The following comment of a director of a not-for-profit organization from an interview that I did best captures the sentiment (Sendjaya, 2015, p. 37):

> I think you can do exactly the same thing with sex. I mean sex is fantastic, it's the perfect expression of love. But you can commercialize it, you can twist it, and you can make it a very ugly aspect. Just look at child prostitution for example. Similarly, work is an excellent concept through which one could express his or her talents to the full, but you can twist it too. Think about workaholism. The principle of servanthood is a wonderful concept, but you can turn it into slavery. It's taking something that is pure and good, and twisting it. And I think you can do that with anything.

In my experience I have been asked in a number of occasions by corporate clients who are interested to undertake the servant leadership training program to alter the word 'servant' into something that is more politically correct. Invariably I would nod in agreement with them and quip, 'Okay, let's not use *servant leadership*. Instead let's roll with *slave leadership*!' The next time someone labels you a servant of Christ, treat that as a condescending remark then tell the person off, 'Who do you think you are to call me a servant! I am not a servant. I am a slave of Christ!'

Embracing a 'humble servant' identity when you are a leader is not a denigrating idea, as some might erroneously think. Christian leaders who understand that they are being called by Christ, the Servant of servants, will learn that when they adopt the servant identity, they follow in the footsteps of Christ.

Self-serving vs. other-serving leaders

Embracing a servant identity is hard, particularly for people who are appointed or called to be leaders. However, as I argued before, selfless service is the hallmark of true leadership (Sendjaya, 2015). Foster (1989) described leadership as a revolutionary act of will to voluntary abandon one's self to others, or simply 'voluntary subordination'.

Voluntary subordination signifies the leader's conviction to renounce the superior status and privileges attached to leadership in order to embrace greatness by way of servanthood. This willingness to abandon self in service to others was exemplified most clearly in the leadership of Jesus Christ. Against the social expectation of the 1st-century Palestine where a servant or a lowest-ranking guest is expected to wash the dusty feet of the people who gathered for a meal, Jesus took the initiative to wash the disciples' feet. His intention was not to highlight the importance of the foot-washing ceremony, but the readiness of leaders to set aside their ego in order to serve others wholeheartedly (cf. John 13:1–16).

The operative word 'voluntary' suggests that the leaders subordinate themselves because they want to, not because they have to. The decision to serve others stem from a willing heart, signifying a conscious and deliberate choice. This notion of subordinating ourselves to others is subversive in contemporary organizations for obvious reasons. Every cell in our bodies screams against the idea of subordinating ourselves to others. Modern people have long embraced that people are created equal, as such they should enjoy the freedom to pursue our natural inclination to get ahead of others. We respond with a hearty amen to that declaration, and would pursue and defend it at all costs. That is why finding even a leader with authentic, selfless service is like finding a needle in a haystack.

If we are honest to ourselves, we often serve other people under one of the following three conditions: When we are in the mood of doing so, when we cannot find an excuse not to, and when it makes us look good. In fact the act of service can be misappropriated or even manufactured to serve one's end. It is not too far-fetched to say that there are fake service and authentic service. How can we tell then if we are truly embracing a servant identity or are chameleons who cleverly shape-shift into a servant-like character for political or social expediency? The following table shows the contrast between self-serving leaders and other-serving leaders.

Self-serving leaders serve others with a distorted motive. They pick and choose areas of service that are too substantial to be ignored by others as a means to expedite their personal ambition or agenda. They would call a press conference for each act of service rendered to maximize the return on service. They tactfully

Table 3.1 Differences between self-serving leaders and other-serving
leaders

	Self-serving Leaders 'Sacrificing others, serving self'	Other-serving Leaders 'Sacrificing self, serving others'
Why	Spend much effort to strategize the service that attracts most attention	Serve as it flows naturally from the heart
Who	Choose individuals to serve based on the potential return	Welcome every genuine opportunity to serve within reason
When	Serve after calculating the result, always requiring external reward	Serve because it is right, resting contented in hiddenness
How	Are affected by moods, service is done only when convenient	Serve because there is a legitimate need as part of an ingrained lifestyle

serve the powerful individuals in the organization in view of the
favors they would receive in the future. They might volunteer to
serve the marginalized people, but only to project a humble image
to the public. For self-serving leaders, the willingness to serve is
dictated by their moods – physical fatigue, emotional strain, relational problems, or even inadequate sleep will throw them off
balance. In short, as service is a matter of convenience rather than
commitment, it is used merely as a means to an end.

In contrast, other-serving leaders are more conscious of their
responsibilities than their rights, readily taking up opportunities to
serve others whenever there is a legitimate need regardless of the
nature of the service, the person served, or the mood of the leader
and without seeking acknowledgement or compensation. Notice
that it says 'a legitimate need', not every single need that arises,
for as limited and created human beings, leaders cannot possibly
meet every single need they find around them. But for every legitimate need God sends their way, they would engage in service self-
sacrificially without much cost-and-benefit analysis.

The acid test of servanthood

How do we know if we have embraced the identity of a servant? When we serve the very individuals whom we know with certainty that they do not have the capacity to return the favor to us. Writing in the 19th century, Spurgeon (1877, p. 373) surmised that it is the most important test of one's character:

> I think you may judge a man's character by the persons whose affection he seeks. If you find a man seeking only the affection of those who are great, depend upon it he is ambitious and self-seeking; but when you observe that a man seeks the affection of *those who can do nothing for him, but for whom he must do every-thing*, you know that he is not seeking himself but that pure benevolence sways his heart.

The second test of our servanthood lies in our instinctive response when we are treated as a servant. Our knee-jerk reaction when we *perceive* that our rights are being trampled upon by someone speaks volumes about our perception of selves. Think about the last time how you responded to people whom you perceive undermined your expertise, experience, or opinion. If we feel offended and engage in defensive mechanisms to protect our ego, we are most likely struggling with our identity as servants.

Does that mean that Christian leaders who embrace the servant identity should allow themselves to be treated as doormats? Absolutely not. We should not let the biblical, grace-filled nature of servanthood be abused. The notion of accountability sheds light on this very concern. We should seek to be accountable not only to the people we serve, but also to others, including the board of directors, governmental authorities, other organizational stakeholders, and the leader's personal core values and moral integrity. Our ultimate accountability, however, is to God, the sovereign judge of the universe.

As such, the Christian leaders' accountability towards their followers is relative, not absolute, lest they turned themselves into panderers who would say or do just about anything to please their followers. There are accountability structures and relationships they consciously put themselves in. The interplay between account-ability and service is perhaps best captured by the phrase 'I am your servant, but you are not my master.' The apostle Paul, for example, regarded himself as the servant of the Corinthians (cf. 1 Corinthians 4:1–4), but the Corinthians were not his master.

Leading servants

We have thus far delineated how Christian leaders could embrace either the 'powerful leader' or 'humble servant' identity. Both options have their respective assumptions and implications when leaders assume positions of power or service. However, these options do not have to be mutually exclusive.

The final important point I want to get across in this chapter is as follows. Christian leaders do not have to choose between the leader or the servant identity. The Gospel enables them to be both, simul-taneously leaders and servants.

But note that they are first and foremost servants of Christ, who were called to do his bidding to lead others. They are *leading servants*, rather than servant leaders. That is, servant is the opera-tive word and leading is the qualifier. They are servants of Christ first, before they are leaders of the people.

I am mindful that the coexistence of servanthood and leadership is seemingly absurd. At the surface it sounds oxymoronic, but fur-ther scrutiny would reveal that it is more of a paradox than an oxy-moron. An oxymoron is a contradiction in terms whereas a paradox is a simultaneous presence of contradictory elements that forms a profound understanding of something new.

In this case, that 'something' is a new understanding of gospel-centered leadership where leading servants in obedience to the calling of Christ engage the rational, relational, practical, emo-tional, and spiritual dimensions of the followers, so much so that when they work together, they are both transformed into what they are capable of becoming.

We learned that the apostles, who were no doubt the leaders of the early church, preferred to refer to themselves individually as 'doulos Christo', or a slave of Christ. That was a peculiar preference given that both the Greek and the Jews at the time found that the notion of slaves was repugnant. The Greek boasted their personal dignity in the fact that they were free, while the Jews considered 'slave' as a denigrating insult one could hurl at another and were known to begin their prayers as 'I thank you God that I am not a slave' (Kittel, Bromiley, & Friedrich, 1964). But despite their role as leaders of the church, the apostles' preferred self-identity were slaves, as evident in the following texts.

> 'Paul, a slave of Christ Jesus, called to be an apostle and set apart for the gospel of God'
>
> (Romans 1:1)

> 'James, a slave of God and of the Lord Jesus Christ'
>
> (James 1:1)

> 'Simon Peter, a slave and apostle of Jesus Christ'
>
> (2 Peter 1:1)

> 'Jude, a slave of Jesus Christ and a brother of James'
>
> (Jude 1:1)

> 'Paul and Timothy, slaves of Christ Jesus'
>
> (Phil 1:1)

Most notably, in his letter to the Corinthians, the apostle Paul wrote that he and his comrades were merely slaves of Christ. Yet, they were also stewards of the mysteries of God (1 Corinthians 4:1–4). As such, they were on the one hand servants of Christ, and on the other hand leaders entrusted by God with an invaluable resource (i.e., the Gospel).

The word 'steward' originates from a Greek word '*oikosnomos*' from which we derived the term 'economy'. It refers to the idea of a household or estate manager. What Paul had in mind was the highest-ranking slave of a wealthy landowner. He was still a slave by status and subject to his master. Yet, he was put in charge of the entire estate in his master's absence, a highly strategic position to oversee other people and direct the day-to-day affairs. The steward had authority over the estate, but only within the boundaries of the will of the lord of the estate. The notion of stewardship is a pervasive theme in the Bible. In the Old Testament, Adam and Eve had authority over the resources in the natural world surrounding them. Their mandate was to manage (not own) God's resources and grow them in God's way and for God's glory.

Such is a Christian leader in front of Christ and his people. They are trusted with an important position of leadership to grow God's resources (i.e., the Gospel) among the people of God, and will be accountable to God for their leadership. Christian leaders are both slaves and rulers. As slaves, they are unconditionally and completely accountable to their master. Every decision and action they make as leaders are done ultimately for the sake of their master, not themselves. Yet they are also leaders who are tasked with managing and growing each and every individual entrusted under their care, lest they are judged as wicked and lazy slaves (Matthew 25:26). In God's economy, service and power are not polar opposites.

Inferiority and superiority

How does the Gospel help Christian managers, supervisors, or pastors have a rock-solid identity in Christ as both leaders and servants? Many who embrace the 'powerful leader' identity often feel superior to others, and many who embody the 'humble servant' identity feel inferior to others.

Morality and religiosity exacerbate that predisposition in our hearts to be superior or inferior. At the center of morality and religiosity is the reliance on self to achieve what our significant others expect of us (society or God, respectively), which typically leads to disdain of others. If we are religious, the more we rely on our own efforts to procure God's blessings, the more likely we oscillate back and forth between superiority ('I am better than others, have done more than others!') and inferiority ('Compared to others, I haven't done enough for God'). Unlike morality or religiosity, the gospel prevents us from ever feeling superior or inferior to others. Consider the following two-pronged truth of the Gospel.

You are not a legend. You are a sinner saved by grace. All your achievements will be forgotten in two generations, three at the most. Even the world's giants, given enough time, will be nothing but a negligible footnote in history. Your sins are so great that Jesus Christ had to die to atone for them. Never feel superior about yourself.

Yet you are not mass produced. You are not even a limited edition. You are one of a kind in this world, a masterpiece of God. You are individually customized for a specific purpose he wants you to achieve. You are so loved that Jesus Christ was willing to die for you. Never feel inferior about yourself.

The extent to which you hold both sides of the Gospel in a creative tension will help you to rightly enjoy people's praises without being succumbed into pride (not feeling superior), and wisely deal with people's criticisms without being sucked into despair (not feeling inferior).

In his presence, we will realize that he is such a holy and awesome God that we and our significant others become comparatively tiny and insignificant human beings. If we come to God merely with admission of limitation and a plea for help, that would trivialize the great gap that exists between us and God. The Gospel comes to us and says, 'You are not only limited and weak. You are a great sinner with deceitful hearts, unclean lips, and corrupt minds.'

On the other hand, it is equally too trivial to come to God and expect to have a spiritual insight or divine inspiration from him. We often treat God like an energy drink, using him to get the strength we need to achieve the outcome we want. The Gospel comes to us and says, 'More than being merely empowered, you will be fundamentally and thoroughly changed from the inside out. You will be reborn as a new creature, and Jesus will be reproduced in you.'

As such, both our admission and ambition are too menial, too insignificant in the face of the gospel. The false teachers will always say to us, 'You can if you think you can. You're a great star!', but the gospel always tells us, 'You can't even if you think you can. You're a great sinner.' The false teachers will always say, 'Have faith in yourself, you are destined for greatness. No one will be able to stop you, let them see the mighty and glorious Y.O.U!' But the gospel always tells us, 'Have faith in Christ, you are created to manifest his greatness. Everyone will stop and stoop one day, when they see you are being transformed into his image from glory to glory.'

Slaves of others for Jesus' sake

When the gospel grips the heart of Christian leaders, the resulting attitude is unmistakably clear. They are willing to call themselves not only slaves to Christ, but also slaves to others. That is a beautifully counterintuitive stance that Christian leaders take towards others. The quintessential of Christian leadership lies in this otherworldly principle once declared by the apostle Paul and his fellow leaders: 'Ourselves as your slaves for Jesus' sake' (2 Corinthians 4:5).

Ministering to the Corinthian church filled with freedom-maximizing believers fascinated with man-made wisdom rather than the pure gospel of the crucified Christ, Paul had to discuss at length how Christians should exercise their freedom (1 Corinthians 8:1–11:1). The entire section on that subject concludes with the injunction: 'Follow me, as I follow Christ' (1 Corinthians 11:1). He implied that the principle and strategy he expounded and lived, which he learned from the Lord, was not exclusively reserved for the apostles, but for all believers of all shapes and forms, particularly those who are called to be Christian leaders.

The repeated usage of the word 'winning' more people to Christ in 1 Corinthians 9 is curious. For Paul, the issue is not about proselytizing people from religion A to religion B. It is about getting people out of the vicious cycle of serving idols into serving the living and true God (1 Thessalonians 1:9). Paul understood that there is a huge gap between God and sinners, and it is a personal issue for God because He stands at one end of that gap. So grave is his concern that God sent his only son to stand in the gap, living the life we should have lived and dying the death we should have had. In many ways, Christian leaders are called to do the same. The content of God's heart has gripped Paul's, and it should have gripped ours too.

In that light, his approach is one that is so peculiar even to the people of his day. He wrote, 'I have made myself a slave to all, that I might win more of them' (1 Corinthians 9:19). Paul, a highly educated, most religious, and free Roman citizen, summarized his life in the following, 'I have become all things to all people, that by all means I might save some (9:23). What he meant was not adopting a lifestyle of moral and doctrinal compromise, for that would contradict what he wrote in the previous chapters (e.g., 'Flee from sexual immorality' – 1 Corinthians 6:18) and doctrinal teaching (e.g., bodily resurrection – 1 Corinthians 15). No second guessing with these absolutes. But when it comes to non-moral and non-doctrinal issues, he went out of his depth to become all things to all people by surrendering his personal rights. The word 'rights' is the second key word repetitively mentioned in that chapter. Paul was saying that even though he and his comrades had certain rights in Christ, the love of Christ compelled them to forsake them so that they could win more to Christ.

In an emotionally-charged defense before his ungrateful critics at Corinth who questioned his ministry, he laid out his personal rights to be appreciated as an apostle of Jesus Christ, to be financially supported, to have a spouse who is also financially supported, and to be freed from working for a living so he can devote his time exclusively for the Gospel ministry (9:1–6).

He then proceeded by giving five compelling reasons in support of those rights from Scripture and common sense that forever silenced his critics who should have known better (9:7–14). Paul in essence exclaimed, 'C'mon Corinthians, use your common sense, read your Scripture, be fair, know your religious tradition, and remember Christ's command. And you will know that I don't pluck these rights out of thin air!'

But Paul did not stop there, for the whole point of airing his rights in public was to set an example for others that he did not cling to any of those rights, let alone maximize them (9:15). Instead he surrendered his rights to Christ and endured anything rather than putting 'an obstacle in the way of the gospel of Christ' (9:12b).

The most effective leadership approach (as it is true in mission, evangelism, and other areas of the Christian ministry within and beyond the church walls) has nothing to do with abundant financial resources or meticulously-run programs. As useful as they might be, the most effective approach has to do with renouncing our personal rights to Christ.

I am cognizant, however, of the difficulty of readily accepting the idea of foregoing our rights. Many Christian leaders fiercely guard their personal rights. They think it is fundamentally wrong for someone to neglect his or her unalienable rights (life, liberty, pursuit of happiness). At the faintest hint that their rights have been unappreciated, disregarded, or violated, they bathe in self-pity and sinful anger. It is not uncommon to hear churches split or the Christian testimony in the workplace spoiled because Christian leaders insist on their rights.

How can we follow Paul as he followed Christ? We cannot and will never be able. Not if we rely on our own leadership experience, wisdom, talents, or strengths. To forego these rights is a supernatural act of worship that necessitates the power of the Gospel to work within us. We are enabled to become all things to all people when we turn our eyes upon Jesus Christ who had become all things to you and me. 'Though he was in the form of God . . . [he] made himself nothing, taking a form of a servant, being born in the likeness of men. And being found in human form, he humbled himself by becoming obedient to the point of death, even death on the cross' (Philippians 2:6–8).

Jesus is not a shepherd leader who merely leads and guides us. He is the shepherd leader who becomes a sheep. He is the lamb that takes away the sin of the world. He is the Leading Servant who leads us sacrificially and dies as a final and ultimate sacrifice, not so that we are exempted from it, but so that we are enabled to do the same in his strength and for his glory.

'Jars of clay' theory of leadership

Christian leaders can be highly charismatic, eloquent, talented, experienced, and skilled, but none of these attributes are uniquely 'Christian'. Contrary to popular understanding, these things that otherwise make up great leadership can be major obstacles of God's working in and through you. It's not that these positive attributes are wrong in and of themselves, but they can be the very things that turn you to seek your glory instead of God's, to rely on your might rather than God's, and to run your agenda rather than God's. Church history is replete with cases of such leaders.

God is still calling leaders today, but he expects the glory for which, the strength with which, and the agenda for which the leaders are called to be his and his alone. Talents, skills, and experience are secondary in his economy. Admission of weakness is primary.

In fact, divine power in human weakness is his modus operandi. We read in the gospels and the book of Acts that he called both the mighty Paul and the shallow Peter, the two leading apostles of the early church with starkly opposite backgrounds, talents, and personalities. But they were useful in his kingdom only when they, despite their many talents or lack of talents, finally admitted that they were nothing before God. The worthless jars of clay must remain worthless for the invaluable gospel treasure within to shine through.

God's pattern from the birth of the world to the re-birth of man has been to create something out of nothing ('Let light shine out of darkness'), through which he and he alone gets the glory. In a similar vein God only uses leaders who see themselves as nobody, so he can turn them into somebody. As long as you remain nobody, he will continue to use you as instruments in his sovereign hands, for that would make him look glorious.

The reverse also makes God look glorious, turning leaders who think they are somebody into nobody. That would unmistakably show that he is the sovereign God who could raise up leaders, put them in power, remove them, and install their successors. God however cannot and will not use those who think they are 'somebody' into a bigger and better version of themselves. It makes him look mediocre and requires his glory to be shared with others. In short, while aspiring to be somebody is a vital strategy to succeed in the kingdom of this world, it is a fatal recipe for failure in the kingdom of God. If we want to be useful in his kingdom, we need to learn to remain nobody.

That is why God sends regular reminders to jog our memories that we are not extraordinary human beings; rather we are merely unadorned clay pots of very ordinary individuals. Without these reminders, the expiration date of your usefulness as instruments in his hands is closer than you think. God in fact has a reputation of driving his servants to the point of frustration. It is not uncommon for them to cry out to their master, 'Who is sufficient for these things?' as they go through work conflicts, financial mishaps, relationship breakdowns, emotional pains, physical suffering, or any combination of the above. But rest assured that for his beloved, every crushing experience is custom-designed by a wise and loving potter who is shaping a better fitting clay to carry the precious treasure of the gospel.

Needless to say, if you are full of self, there is no room left for that treasure. Thus, you have to be empty of self. Empty of self-sufficiency, self-love, self-importance. In these self-emptying experiences lies the answer to the question: Who then is sufficient for gospel ministry? No one is. But with the apostle Paul, we should positively respond to God's calling hastily adding 'not that we are sufficient in ourselves to claim anything as coming from us, but our sufficiency is from God' (2 Corinthians 3:5).

References

Alger, Jr., H. (1883). *Abraham Lincoln, the backwoods boy* (p. 304). New York, NY: American Publishers Corporation.

Ashforth, B. E., & Schinoff, B. S. (2016). Identity under construction: How individuals come to define themselves in organizations. *Annual Review of Organizational Psychology and Organizational Behavior*, 3, 111–137.

Bartel, C., & Dutton, J. (2001). Ambiguous organizational memberships: Constructing organizational identities in interactions with others. In M. A. H. A. D. J. Terry (Ed.), *Social identity processes in organizational contexts* (pp. 115–130). Philadelphia: Psychology Press.

Bennett, D. W. 1998. *Leadership images from the New Testament.* Carlisle, UK: OM Publishing.

Campbell, W. K., Bonacci, A. M., Shelton, J., Exline, J. J., & Bushman, B. J. (2004). Psychological entitlement: Interpersonal consequences and validation of a self-report measure. *Journal of Personality Assessment*, 83, 29–45.

Ciulla, J. B. (1995). Leadership ethics: Mapping the territory. *Business Ethics Quarterly*, 5(1), 5–25.

DeRue, D. S., & Ashford, S. J. (2010). Who will lead and who will follow? A social process of leadership identity construction in organizations. *Academy of Management Review*, 35(4), 627–647.

Foster, R. J. (1989). *Celebration of discipline.* London: Hodder & Stoughton.

Getz, G. A. 1984. *Serving one another.* Wheaton, IL: Victor.

Hannah, S. T., Woolfolk, R. L., & Lord, R. G. (2009). Leader self-structure: A framework for positive leadership. *Journal of Organizational Behavior*, 30(2), 269–290.

Harris, M. J. (1999). *Slave of Christ.* Downers Grove, IL: InterVarsity Press.

Harvey, P., & Martinko, M. J. (2009). An empirical examination of the role of attributions in psychological entitlement and its outcomes. *Journal of Organizational Behavior*, 30, 459–476.

Kets De Vries, M. F. R. (1993). *Leaders, fools, and impostors: Essays on the psychology of leadership.* San Francisco: Jossey-Bass.

Kittel, G., Bromiley, G. W., & Friedrich, G. (1964). *Theological dictionary of the New Testament* (Chapter 2, p. 261). Grand Rapids, MI: Eerdmans.

Lewis, C. S. (1952). *Mere Christianity.* New York: Macmillan Publication.

Locyker, H. 1986. *Nelson's Illustrated Bible Dictionary.* Nashville, TN: Thomas Nelson.

Lord, R. G., & Maher, K. J. (1991). *Leadership and information processing: Linking perceptions and performance.* Boston: Unwin Hyman.

Luther, M. (1943). *Christian liberty.* Philadephia: Muhlenberg (First published 1520).

Markus, H., & Wurf, E. (1987). The dynamic self-concept: A social psychological perspective. *Annual Review of Psychology*, 38, 299–337.

Robertson, A. & Plummer, A. 1911. *A critical and exegetical commentary on the first epistele of St Paul to the Corinthians*. Edinburgh: T. and T. Clark.

Sendjaya, S. (2005). Morality and leadership: Examining the ethics of transformational leadership. *Journal of Academic Ethics, 3,* 75–86.

Sendjaya, S. (2015). *Personal and organizational excellence through servant leadership*. Springer International.

Spurgeon, C.H. (1877). *The metropolitan tabernacle pulpit: Sermons*. New York: Passmore & Alabaster.

Sveningsson, S. F., & Alvesson, M. (2003). Managing managerial identities: Organizational fragmentation, discourse and identity struggle. *Human Relations, 56,* 1163–1193.

Thayer, J. 1996. *Thayer's Greek-English Lexicon of the New Testament* (Reissue ed.). Peabody, MA: Hendrickson Publishers.

Tjosvold, D., & van Knippenberg, B. M. (2009). *Power and interdependence in organizations*. Cambridge, UK: Cambridge University.

Vine, W. E. 1985. *Vine's Expository Dictionary of Biblical Words*. Nashville, TN: Thomas Nelson.

CHAPTER 4

When leaders run on the performance treadmill

*'As I have a position in the world, keep me from
making the world my position;
may I never seek in the creature what can
be found only in the Creator'*
(*from a prayer from the Valley of
Vision entitled 'A Disciple's Renewal'*)

Moritz Erhardt, a twenty-one-year old intern at Bank of America Merrill Lynch was found dead in the bathroom of his shared accommodation in London, England, at 8:30pm on 15 August 2014. The coroner who investigated the case concluded that his death was triggered by a prolonged lack of sleep, which resulted in an epileptic seizure (Kennedy, 2013). He allegedly worked seventy-two hours without sleep prior to that.

Erhardt was described as a talented, hardworking, high-performing, and well-liked intern who was coming to the end of a seven-week summer internship worth £6,000 with the bank. With his heart fully set on securing a full-time position at the bank after graduation, he tried to impress his employer by working three days and nights in a row, a ritual in investment banking known as the 'magic-roundabout'. The phrase refers to the practice of employees like Erhardt calling a cab from the office to their apartments in the early hours of the morning around 4am or 5am, and asking the cab driver to wait while they have a quick shower, put on a fresh shirt, and head back to the office (Day, 2013). Erhardt was used to theworking long hours, but pulling three successive all-nighters with 21-hour stints each day is certainly above the expectations.

His father, a psychoanalyst, remarked during an interview that Erhardt was aware of the intense work culture, and his fatherly advice to take it easy fell into deaf ears. In fact, Erhardt enjoyed the endorphin rush he experienced there, much akin to mountaineers who persist at climbing higher despite doing so on low oxygen. He did not blame the bank for exploiting his son; in his view it was Erhardt who was exploiting himself (Day, 2013). The irony of this tragedy is unbeknownst to Erhardt; even before that fateful 72-hour period the bank had prepared to make an offer to Erhardt for a full-time analyst position after graduation with a £45,000 starting salary.

Most leaders know that working extremely long hours poses a lethal danger to their physical, mental, and emotional wellbeing, but they typically ignore it at their own peril. Executives liken that intense work as an adrenaline rush that is irresistible and addictive (Hewlett & Carolyn, 2006). For those who experience it on a regular basis however, they no longer see it as a form of temporary insanity but a new normal that significantly contributes to their sense of importance, worth, and identity.

While these are found in certain industries more than others, this identity-forming craze is typical of even young achievers in various industries, who see all-nighters as a badge of honor so they can brag in the morning to their colleagues about the long hours and to their boss they have what it takes to succeed (Malik, 2013). It is in the name of personal success that Erhardt became engulfed in what is known as the *principle of potentiality*, which states that one is capable of becoming always more than what she or he is, as the following commentary below elucidates (Costea, Watt, & Amiridis, 2015):

> What he seems to have succumbed to is a mentality whose ground is that he can hold and live in the name of the idea that he has no limits, that there is always 'more' to be brought out, actualized, from the plenitude of his potential. Erhardt did not feel complete, formed, full – he rather seems to have felt compelled by, and towards, a far more dangerous horizon: a horizon

through which managerialism has succeeded to represent work as a form of ultimate self-empowerment, self-expression, and self-realization.

While many concluded that it was Erhardt himself who sealed his fate, it was obvious that it was exacerbated by the performance culture in which he operated. Jeff Immelt, the previous CEO of General Electric (GE), which is perhaps the most consistently high-performing global firms on earth with practices and policies that other firms always try to replicate, highlights the importance of maintaining the performance management culture. The fast-paced business landscape that GE operates in means that they have to do it even more vigorously (Immelt, 2015).

> My notion is we're in a permanently complex world. And this historical organization chart with lots of processes is a thing of the past. We've basically unplugged anything that was annual. The notion is that, in the digital age, sitting down once a year to do anything is weird, it's just bizarre. So whether it's doing business reviews or strategic planning, it's in a much more continuous way.
>
> We still give a lot of feedback. We still do a lot of analysis of how you're performing. But we make it much more contemporary and much more 360-degree. So somebody can get interactions with their boss on a monthly basis or a quarterly basis. And the data you get is being collected by your peers, the people who work for you, in a much more accurate and fluid way

The intensity of performance management culture is perfectly rational given the fixation on growth and performance. In such context, however, many businesses sacrifice people on the altar of profit. Individual employees are treated as units of production or expendable resources in a profit and loss statement. 'The business of business is business', 'Greed is good', 'Only the paranoid survives', and other similar mantras are so entrenched they become a pretext for businesses that hope to thrive.

No wonder the wise prognosis that management guru Peter Drucker reportedly uttered becomes a strange voice in the wilderness:

'Profit is to a corporation what oxygen for the human body; necessary for its existence, but not the reason for it.'

▓ The relationship between performance and identity

Countless leaders are living by a work-life dynamic pattern not dissimilar to, though less extreme than, that shown by Erhardt. They regard their leadership performance, either the intensity of their efforts or the quality output, as a way to validate themselves, hence forming an important part of their identity.

As discussed in the previous chapter, identity is a major fundamental construct in the field of human behavior study that explains why we think about our surroundings and how we respond to stimuli in those surroundings (Ashforth & Mael, 1989).

Often what we do and why we do it on a daily basis is a function of our identity. Identity matters because it is the process by which we define ourselves, and work typically has a major influence in that process (e.g., membership of a certain organization, association with a certain cause, achievements in certain fields, possession of traits that fit certain professions, etc.).

Organizational identity scholars argue that the core attributes of identity are made up of cognitive and affective elements. Our cognitive side says, 'I am A, I value A' (because it's important to me), whereas our affective side says 'I feel about A'. What one perceives and feels as essential will be self-defining in that one changes to become more similar to the role he or she is occupying. For example, if that same woman in the foregoing example says, 'I am a managing partner in a global management consulting firm, I enjoy achieving success in my management consulting career, and that is important to me,' that is largely because she thinks and feels her way into identification. That essentially means that she finds sources of pride in her role and tends to feel positive about her identification with the role and achieving well in that role. Specifically, the prestige associated with both the role and the firm is reflected onto her as a prominent and senior member of the firm.

In fact, in order to be a better representative of that role category, she would envision what a highly performing managing partner does and looks like, and strive to achieve that ideal. That basic motive for identifying with a role, according to the social identity theory, is enhancement of one's sense of self-esteem. In other words, she does not only allow her role to define her, but she would intentionally and systematically promote the perception that the role makes her a more worthwhile individual (Ashforth, Harrison, & Corley, 2008).

Classic social psychology studies such as Zimbardo's Stanford Prison experiment show the deep-seated psychological effects of role internalization (Zimbardo, 2007). In 1971 Professor Philip Zimbardo of Stanford University conducted an experiment involving twenty-four students with stable and healthy psychological profiles who were recruited as participants of the two-week prison simulation.

Half of the participants were randomly assigned the roles of prison guards and the other half, prisoners. The entire experiment took place in small mock prison cells in the basement of the Stanford University's psychology building. The guards were provided with clothing similar to actual prison guard uniforms as well as wooden batons and mirrored sunglasses, whereas prisoners were given ill-fitting smocks and stocking caps, chained around one ankle, and assigned prison numbers as a new identity by which they would be addressed by the guards. While the guards can go home after their eight-hour shifts, prisoners were told to remain in their cells (and occasionally the prison yard) throughout the experiment.

The experiment barely passed one day when things started to go awry. The prisoners thought the guards were too aggressive in the experiment and refused their instructions, which made the guards behave in increasingly aggressive behaviors. Following several incidents involving prisoners' hunger strike and solitary confinement, the guards' behaviors escalated from aggressive to sadistic. Understandably many prisoners experienced deep emotional trauma.

The experiment went out of control so quickly that it was abruptly halted after only six days. The guards made the plea to continue the experiment. In his response to critics of the experiment, Zimbardo concluded that his experiment 'serves as a cautionary tale of what might happen to any of us if we underestimate the extent to which the power of social roles and external pressures can influence our actions'.[1]

The simulated-prison experiment might be an extreme demonstration of role internalization that can never be replicated due to its seriously dubious ethics (in fact, a major overhaul of the ethical guidelines for experiments involving human subjects was conducted in the United States following the experiment). However, we display a much milder form of role internalization in our daily lives. This proclivity to allow our professional roles to define who we are can be observed most readily when we do self-introduction at work or social function.

Think about the last time you did that, perhaps it was a conference where you met new faces who might be potential clients, or a birthday party of a friend of your child. What typically came up in the conversation after you mention your name is what you do, which includes your formal title and your employer. Often your response will be used as a gauge by which the other individual decides whether you are worth continuing the conversation with.

As such, your response becomes a proxy of your perceived self-worth. To say that you are a senior partner of a global consulting firm, for example, is more likely to create a wow effect on the other individual, hence might boost our self-esteem. On the contrary, to admit that you have been in-between jobs for the last twelve months would be quite embarrassing for you, hence might damage your self-image. This otherwise menial social gesture speaks volumes to the fact that our identity is often based on what we do rather than who we are.

■ Improving self-worth on a performance treadmill

Left unchecked, many aspiring and seasoned leaders can be easily trapped on a performance treadmill that they inadvertently created in order to construct a certain identity of self. This tendency is so pervasive among young leaders who feel like they have to prove themselves to the world.

The overwhelming majority of them today belong to what has become to be known as the millennial generation. Though often criticized as a crude generalization or stereotype, repeated studies have shown that millennials are characterized by fixation with self-improvement in many areas from career to body shape. They perpetually see a perceived gap between how they are doing and how they think they could be doing, hence are overly critical when it comes to their own performance self-assessment (Anderson, Baur, Griffith, & Buckley, 2017).

One of the millennials' cultural icons, Lady Gaga, whose global popularity affords her a huge influence on millions of her fans, is a case in point. I am fully aware that perhaps she will not be the first person who comes to mind when we think of a leader. But if we subscribe to the one-word, albeit very loose, definition of leadership as influence, she certainly fits the bill as an incredibly successful leader. Her story is one that many leaders can relate to because her deep struggle with her identity and performance is one that is often experienced by many, particularly those who are very good at what they do or aspiring to always be very good.

Growing up being bullied by her school friends, who laughed at her appearance, Gaga made a vow to work extremely hard to prove them wrong. At the pinnacle of her success as a mega superstar however, she cannot escape that nagging sense of insecurity. Journalists comment how her edgy performances and dress sense are merely a mask for her insecurity. The following comment that she gave at an interview with HBO in 2011 captures that sentiment:[2]

> I start to think about all the people that have tried to stop me, and I get this, like, super-intense fury. Yeah, then I think about how I don't give a s*** if people don't understand what I do, as long as I my fans understand . . .
>
> I just sometimes feel like a loser still, you know? It's crazy because it's like we're at the Garden but I still sometimes feel like a loser kid in high school. I've just to pick my s*** up, I've got to pick myself up, and I have to tell myself I'm a superstar every morning so that I can get through this day and be for my fans what they need for me to be . . . But sometimes I still feel like people are trying to destroy me. I cannot be destroyed, I will not be destroyed and you will never destroy the kingdom that is my fans.

On that throne of the kingdom of fans is sitting the god of performance who is worshipped not only by millennials but also by many from other generational cohorts in the four corners of the earth.

The incessant need to improve and prove one's self is exacerbated by cultural features such as face-saving. Research using data from the National Longitudinal Study of Adolescent Health in the US shows an unexpected link between self-esteem and academic performance. The study found that the ethnic group with the lowest self-esteem in the United States is Asian Americans, yet it is also the group with the strongest academic performance (Bankston & Zhou, 2002).

The explanation of this finding lies in the face-saving culture. Low self-esteem is the fuel for high performance. While it is often lauded as a positive feature of the Asian culture, it may also signal a chronic addiction to high performance. Individuals who are raised in that culture were typically hardwired to perfect their areas of competency in order to secure the accolades of the family and subsequently the world (or stated more negatively, to save one's and the family's face).

When insecure overachievers worship the god of performance

In the achievement-intoxicated culture, overachievers like Lady Gaga tend to think that it is possible to always maintain their level of performance without damaging their mental, emotional, and physical resources in the long run.

High performance is to overachievers what a drink is to alcoholics; they feel disoriented and unworthy when they relax, and address that yearning for perfection by making more sacrifices of their time, energy, relationships, and sanity.

In many ways, overachievers are very religious people with a white-hot zeal for the god of performance. Ardent followers of this god have the innate tendency to be haunted by the myth of their potential, leading them to think that there are always better, bigger, higher, or bolder things that they can do to expand their kingdoms of fans in this world.

Global consulting firms like McKinsey are renowned globally for their deliberate core strategy to hire fresh graduates over experienced consultants. Specifically, they are looking for newly minted MBAs who fall under the category of 'insecure overachievers'. Only the best candidates are hired following a horrendous selection process.

Insecure overachievers are high-performing and fiercely ambitious individuals who are driven by a deep sense of their own inadequacy (Empson, 2017). Typically working as lawyers, investment bankers, management consultants, accountants, they need to prove they are worthy to be part of elite professional organizations. They rely on their performance as validation of their existence. They have a resolute determination to ensure their clients are fully satisfied with their work, even if it means sacrificing their personal well being. Desire for status and fear of failure perpetually compel these young professionals to work harder, smarter, and longer.

The culture of hiring relatively cheaper young and inexperienced consultants while charging clients top dollars is one that is entrenched in many professional firms. They start as interns or junior analysts, working their way up the ladder of the firm to become partners by working up to 125 hours a week, including weekends (Empson, 2017). The extremely long work hours are legendary in professional organizations, and are seen as a badge of honor. Once they are at the top, they would replicate the pattern and demand their staff to emulate it. Repeated studies have shown that the perpetual drive to excel in these arduous work hours can lead to serious physical and mental health problem (e.g., burnout, chronic pain, addictions, eating disorders, depression).

This dangerous pattern is exacerbated by a paradoxical combination of control and autonomy. Elite professional organizations have built a strong culture that acts as social control to ensure staff conformity. Yet professionals feel they are overworking out of their own free choice. That is, they are willing to sacrifice everything to thrive as a coping mechanism of their inadequacy, and if others can do it, the thought of not doing it only further assures them of their perceived inadequacy.

How do individuals become insecure overachievers in the first place? Research shows that this tendency is forged in one's childhood by experiences of psychological, financial, or physical insecurity. Children who experience unexpected poverty might grow up with anxiety and the tenacity to do everything to amass wealth to ensure that poverty only happens in their past. Others are brought up in a context where the only times they will get attention, praise, or love from their parents are when their behaviors and performance exceed the parents' expectations.

Since the root cause of the insecurity is deeply planted in the past, organizational researchers typically suggest remedies that merely address the symptoms. For example, do not let others define what success is for you, refuse the attempts others make to manipulate your anxiety, and respect yourself by savoring each achievement. While helpful, these remedies do not help us to deal with that nagging feeling of inadequacy and anxiety.

The gospel offers a radically different solution. We are more loved by God than we would ever imagine when he sent Jesus, his only Son, to die for us while we were still ignorant of him, and adopted us as his sons and daughters. That knowledge of being noticed and embraced by God in Jesus Christ, the most important Being in the universe, will diminish any fear and guilt of not doing enough to feel worthy.

It was not our worth that prompted Jesus to come and rescue us from ourselves. It was Jesus' sacrificial love that made us worthy. In turn, we will have the motivation to excel, not out of fear or guilt, but out of joy, knowing that my success or failure will not erode his never-stopping, never-giving-up love. Our performance is still important, but has a shift of meaning, from a poor means of covering our inadequacy to a redeemed means to love and serve the One who has loved and served us first. The following sections will expand on this gospel truth.

Christ is our identity

Even Christian leaders are prone to worship the god of performance when achievement is what really matters to them. While they worship Jesus Christ as Lord on Sunday, they might worship their KPIs (key performance indicators) on Monday and merely use Christ as a means to bolster their efforts to meet those KPIs.

There is a huge Sunday-Monday gap, a discrepancy between their espoused theory and theory-in-use that leaves them ineffective as Christian leaders.

They might possess a cognitive mastery of the doctrine of justification by faith and are able to explain it with a high degree of theological precision, but they practice justification by performance in KPIs and merely use Jesus as a means to bolster their efforts to meet or even exceed those KPIs.

In order for Christian leaders to stop worshipping the idol of performance, they need to understand what it means to have their identity rooted in Christ and what differences it makes to the way they operate.

To that end, travel with me back in time to the 1st century Palestinian near the bank of the Jordan River where Jesus was baptized. The story of Jesus' baptism recorded in the Gospel of Matthew is very familiar to many Christians; we lose its deeper meaning. There is more to the account than meets the eye. Outside of crucifixion, the baptism is the only event in Jesus' life mentioned in all four Gospels.

In Matthew chapter 3, we were told that there was a voice from heaven when Jesus was being baptized that served as a confirmation of God's acceptance towards Jesus: 'And behold, a voice from heaven said, "This is my beloved Son, with whom I am well pleased"' (Matthew 3:17).

That affirmation from heaven occurred right before Matthew 4 where Jesus faced the temptations of the devil. This sequence is crucial to understand. Jesus received the heavenly acceptance as the Messianic Son before he fought the temptations. The acknowledgement of the Father's love came before he performed. Acceptance first, performance second. We ought to be thankful the Father's words of affirmation was recorded in Matthew 3, not at the end of Matthew 4 after Jesus passed the temptations with flying colors, or at the end of Matthew 28 after Jesus proved his obedience to the point of death on the cross.

The best commentary of this particular text comes from Henry Nouwen, a Catholic professor and author whose meditations on the Scripture has fed the souls of many throughout generations. Countless times I have been nourished by the crumbs from his table.

His insight on the necessity of drawing on Christ to understand who we are is worth citing at length (Nouwen, 1992, pp. 32–36):

> Yes, there is that voice, the voice that speaks from above and from within and that whispers softly or declares loudly: 'You are my Beloved, on you my favor rests.' It certainly is not easy to hear that voice in a world filled with voices that shout: 'You are no good, you are ugly; you are worthless; you are despicable; you are nobody – unless you can demonstrate the opposite.'
>
> These negative voices are so loud and so persistent that it is easy to believe them. That's the great trap. It is the trap of self-rejection. Over the years, I have come to realize that the greatest trap in our life is not success, popularity, or power, but self-rejection. Success, popularity, and power can indeed present a great temptation, but their seductive quality often comes from the way they are part of the much larger temptation to self-rejection.
>
> When we have come to believe in the voices that call us worthless and unlovable, then success, popularity, and power are easily perceived as attractive solutions. The real trap, however, is self-rejection. As soon as someone accuses me or criticizes me, as soon as I am rejected, left alone, or abandoned, I find myself thinking, 'Well, that proves once again that I am a nobody . . . '
>
> Self-rejection is the greatest enemy of the spiritual life because it contradicts the sacred voice that calls us the 'Beloved.' Being the Beloved constitutes the core truth of our existence . . . We are intimately loved long before our parents, teachers, spouses, children, and friends loved or wounded us. That's the truth of our lives. That's the truth I want you to claim for yourself. That's the truth spoken by the voice that says, 'You are my Beloved.'

It is the acceptance of who he is as God's beloved that enables Jesus to perform well when he was tempted to turn stones into bread after forty days of fasting. Jesus did not need to prove to the Devil or the world that he can do that before he was fully approved by his heavenly Father. In refusing to bow to the temptation, he in essence declared he did not need to perform to become the Son of God.

By virtue of our union with Christ, we have the same acceptance and acknowledgement by the Father the moment we personally trust in Christ. It is as if God looks down from heaven to us and sees each one of us as if we are pure and blameless despite our checkered past. Because of what Christ has done for us on the cross, God can and will also say 'You are my beloved, in whom I am well pleased.' Not only does God overlook those dubious episodes in our lives, but because of Christ, he thinks of us as individuals with perfect record, above reproach in every single area. That is because our lives are now hidden with Christ in God (Colossians 3:3).

The contra-conditional love of God

I would hasten to note however that God's love for us in Christ is not one that is sentimental or romantic. It is common in the Christian vernacular to say 'God accepts you as you are because his love for you is unconditional' to someone who is experiencing the pain of rejection.

Think for example of someone who is being passed up for a promotion or being verbally undermined by his boss. He would appreciate those kind words that are meant to ease the pain. God's unconditional love would be an oasis of comfort that cannot be taken away by his superior or whoever else for that matter. That God's love is unconditional is so antithetical to that of the boss that comes with all sorts of terms and conditions.

A closer scrutiny of those seemingly kind words however might reveal a few potential adverse effects. The emphasis on God's love for us in and of itself will feed our hunger for self-centeredness, validating us incessantly and making us feel perpetually righteous. It propels an attitude of the heart that focuses on the self.

To the employee who did not get the promotion, psychologists would typically recommend him to interrupt his negative, self-limiting thoughts and convince himself of his worth regardless. He would be advised to engage in a self-talk to assure his self-worth, as if he were speaking to his boss. And since he believes in God, the self-talk will go something along this line, 'Hey boss, who are you to treat me like that? You are too insignificant to understand that even God of the Universe treats me like the apple of his eye!'

This psychological self-talk ignores one crucial fact. God has his eye on us because we are united to Jesus, the true apple of God's eye. As such, the self-talk and the accompanying attitude feed our ego, making us feeling superior to others and minimizing the need to come with the humble heart to the throne of grace.

The Gospel tells us that God does not love us unconditionally, but contra-conditionally. That is, God loves us despite all the conditions that prohibit a holy God to love an unholy sinner.

And that is made possible only because of what theologians call the active and passive obedience of Christ. He lived a life of perfect obedience to the moral will of God, and he died a perfect substitutionary death on our behalf. In the absence of this gospel truth, God's accepting us the way we are does sound like a pie in the sky in the harsh reality of the fallen world. It is simply too good to be true.

God's love comes at a great cost to God. It costs him his Son, who had to bear the penalty of our sins on the cross so that the righteousness of Christ can be transferred to us. 'For our sake he made him to be sin who knew no sin, so that in him we might become the righteousness of God' (2 Corinthians 5:21). This life-changing love therefore is not poured onto us out of negligence. When he overlooked our sin, he did not fail to uphold the principle of law and justice that demand just punishment of sins. The death of Christ on the cross occurred precisely to serve that purpose. The following remark aptly explains the contra-conditional love of God (Powlison, 1995, p. 39):

> The Gospel is better than unconditional love. The Gospel says, 'God accepts *you* just as *Christ* is. God has 'contra-conditional' love for you.' Christ bears the curse you deserve. Christ is fully pleasing to the Father and gives you His own perfect goodness. Christ reigns in power, making you the Father's child and coming close to you to begin to change what is unacceptable to God about you.
>
> God never accepts me 'as I am.' He accepts me 'as I am in Jesus Christ.' The center of gravity is different. The true Gospel does not allow God's love to be sucked into the vortex of the

soul's lust for acceptability and worth in and of itself. Rather, it radically decenters people – what the Bible calls 'fear of the Lord' and 'faith' – to look outside ourselves.

What it means for the aspiring leader who did not get the promotion in the aforementioned example is as follows. God loves him regardless of how sinful his thoughts and deeds were done in the past (e.g., using company resources to serve personal agenda, finding scapegoats for a costly blunder he made) or he will be doing in the future (e.g., plotting evil to get even with the boss, strategizing to mentally resign from the job by reducing productivity by 50%). But the only logical reason why God can do that is because Jesus Christ on my behalf has fulfilled every single condition to earn God's love. God accepts him as he is in Christ.

A double-edged sword

The genius of God's contra-conditional love is that it functions like a double-edged sword. On the one hand, God accepts us as we are in Christ. On the other hand, he will not be content leaving us where we are. He wants the recipients of his love to change, and show that evidence of change in their daily lives.

Note that it is entirely different from unconditional love. If God loves us unconditionally, it means that whatever condition we are in at any stage, his love will remain constant regardless. Left to our own sinful nature, we will quickly take that love for granted and render unnecessary any inclination to change our selves. We would say, 'If God loves me no matter what, why bother changing my lifestyle, priorities, habits, etc.?'

It is a familiar scenario we often find in the workplace. Suppose that in order to get things done at work I often bully my staff by giving them unreasonable work demands and making belittling comments to provoke them to up their game. My manager is fully aware of that, but because my team always outperforms the other teams in the entire company, he conveniently turns a blind eye and continually showers me with praise, accolades, and privileges. As such, I have no real incentive to change my toxic attitudes.

Unconditional love is in many respects identical to the notion of unconditional positive regard conceptualized by Carl Rogers. In his theorizing of self-worth, Rogers argued that self-worth is a function of correspondence between our self-image and ideal self (Rogers, 1961). In other words, a healthy self-esteem is one where our feelings, experiences, and behaviors should be consistent with how we see ourselves today (self-image) and in the future (ideal self).

That sense of congruence is determined largely by the so-called unconditional positive regard, which is the total, perpetual, and benign acceptance that we receive from our significant others with no expectation to change whatsoever.

God's love is contra-conditional because his accepting me is based on something that is very costly, namely Christ's sacrifice on the cross. The more we understand that cost, the more we are motivated to change. The more I appreciate the fact that it is my sins that held him on the cross and yet I am the one who gains his reward, the more I am deeply encouraged to stop living for myself and start living for Christ.

As the old hymn goes, 'love so amazing, so divine, demands my soul, my life, my all'. God's love is large enough to simultaneously accept me in Christ *and* expect me to change to become someone who is less like me and more like Christ.

Getting the sequence right: Acceptance (*being*), then performance (*doing*)

I have argued thus far for the futility of having a fixation on our performance as means to validate ourselves. Instead of relying on our performance as a basis of our identity, we have to rely on Christ' performance when he lived the life we cannot possibly live and died the death we should have died.

The extent to which we understand this truth will influence our motivation to perform with excellence for the sake of Christ. As such, the Gospel tells Christian leaders that being accepted by God at a huge cost is the motivational basis for them to excel in their respective roles as leaders.

The sequence with which this occurs in the lives of Christian leaders is important. They first receive that identity-forming acceptance of God in Christ, then they work hard and give 110% in their job as a natural outflow of a life that has been redeemed by Christ. Acceptance (*being*) is followed by performance (*doing*).

A Christian leader who gets the sequence in the wrong order is a disaster waiting to happen. In theology the common fallacy of performing in order to be accepted is commonly called moralistic or legalistic teaching. Moralistic teaching is the core of all religions, including Christianity. It is pervasive in many churches today, typically in Asia where moral performance is upheld as a key virtue given the deeply seated influence of Confucianism, among others.

Religious-moralistic vs. gospel-centered leaders

Unlike liberal views or even cults that bluntly undermine the deity and/or humanity of Christ, moralistic teaching subtly pushes Christ aside either as a moral ideal to emulate ('I want to be like Jesus') or a moral support to enable the attainment of a higher moral ground ('I want to be like King David or apostle Paul').

In the final analysis, moralistic teaching is about me, not Christ. I feel great if I succeed, and I feel worthless when I fail. Moralistic teaching creates pride, anger, fear, guilt, anxiety, and other negative emotions that drive people away from the Gospel. In turn, it makes us numb to the fact that Christians should celebrate every time they open their eyes in the morning, that there is therefore now no condemnation for those who are in Christ Jesus (Romans 8:1).

Those who think salvation as a reward typically overestimate their religious performance in attaining it. Those who know salvation is a gift typically underestimate their religious arrogance in accepting it. Both options are wrought with pride – one says 'I can attain it', the other 'I don't need it'. We all need salvation from yourself, from sin, from Satan, from death, and from hell. We all need Jesus as a Savior (not just as a moral example). But we cannot attain it; the harder we try, the clearer we see its unattainability. Salvation is a gift. We need to stop trying to achieve it and start resting in Christ to receive it.

Indeed, to receive God's rich blessings of salvation, rely on Christ's expense, not ours. That's why it's called GRACE (God's

Riches At Christ's Expense), and not GRAYE (God's Richest at Your Expense).

To paraphrase Marx, the incessant need to perform for God is indeed the opiate of Christians. Perform better, try harder, do more, aim higher, ad infinitum. We think our performance matters. God thinks otherwise. That is why Christ had to become human and perform before God on our behalf. What matters is what Christ has done for us, not what we have to do for him. In fact, it is arrogant to assume that our best intentions and efforts are good enough to satisfy God's standards. If your righteous acts were like filthy rags before we knew Christ, what makes you think they were any different after you knew Christ? If it goes undetected, unassuming Christian leaders might think they are storing the blessing of Christ whilst in fact they are avoiding Christ as their Savior precisely with their morality.

Countless Christian leaders are genuinely misguided in their moralistic behaviors. They erroneously believe that their moral and non-moral performance will secure God's blessings. Note however that the Bible does not teach it. In statistical terms, the correlation between obedience and blessings in the Bible is insignificant. Abraham and Job both obeyed God and showed that first-grace obedience to the fullest extent of their hearts in the most gruesome trials of life. The outcomes are completely mind-boggling. Abraham did not lose his son in the end while Job lost all his children. On the other side of the equation, we also see the same pattern. The correlation between disobedience and loss of blessings is insignificant. Peter and Judas both disobeyed, but Peter was forgiven and Judas was not.

The whole point of these spurious results of obedience, or disobedience, therefore, is twofold. First, we cannot control God with our obedience. We cannot tame God. We cannot bribe him with our moral or non-moral performance. He can and does do whatever he pleases because he is a sovereign God.

Second, it leads us deeper into God. It leads us into thinking, 'What is the point of obeying God, if that does not attract his blessings in return?' Because we now want to get God, rather than his blessings. Because we find his beauty is more ravishing than our bounty, his holiness is now more important than our happiness, his wisdom is more valuable than our wealth. Being transformed into the image of Christ is more valuable than projecting our image onto our CV. Obedience in that sense is no longer transactional. It's not what you get from it but what you become by it that now matters.

To get the point across in simple terms, let us consider Damian and Grace, two Christian colleagues working in the same consulting firm as junior partners. Both of them are in charge of roughly the same number of direct reports and key accounts under their respective portfolio. Brought up in a church steeped in moralistic teaching, Damian believes that God's favor is upon those whose work ethic and integrity is unblemished. His laser-focused attention to work make him appear standoffish and overbearing to others.

Grace has a different approach to work. She believes that because Christ's love shown on the cross for her is sufficient, she does not have prove anything to Christ or to anyone for that matter. While she is also a high-performing partner, she appears more relaxed and contented. She is never worried about who gets the credit when things go well and often becomes the first person to take blame for her team members when things go south. 'If

Table 4.1 The contrast between a moralistic and gospel-centered leader

Dimensions	Damian 'The Religious-Moralist'	Grace 'The Gospel-centered'
How I operate	I perform my best at work for God to secure and maintain his acceptance	Because I have been accepted by God, I want to excel at work for him
How I approach God	Transactional – I obey God for his blessings. The more I obey, the more I am blessed (e.g., success, health, power)	Relational – I obey God for God himself. The more I obey, the more I sense he is real to me
How I treat Jesus	Jesus is useful – he is a great example to follow, and proves to be an effective means to bolster my chances to succeed	Jesus is beautiful – he is a Savior who saves me from my preoccupation with self

(Continued)

Table 4.1 (Continued)

Dimensions	Damian 'The Religious-Moralist'	Grace 'The Gospel-centered'
How I view other people	My office is filled with good people and bad people	My office is filled with sinners who are either aware or unaware of their need of Christ
When I succeed	Pride – my success proves my qualities and hard work, that's why God is on my side	Humility – I can only achieve it through Christ who enables me. All credit is his
When I fail	Despair – God loves those who perform. Now that I've failed, I am not sure whether his favor is still upon me. My guilt eats me alive	Contentment – Failure hurts, but it brings me closer to God, experiencing afresh his grace. I fail yet again, but that won't diminish his love upon me
When others fail	Judgmental – They deserve it, and God knows it. They don't try as hard as I have. It'll be interesting to see whether they can crawl out of their self-made hole	Compassionate – If it were not for God's restraining grace, I might end up much worse. We're all sinners in need of his grace, I'd see what I can do to help
When things go wrong	'God, why didn't you do something? You can't punish me after everything I've done for you! My efforts deserve to be rewarded with a good life'	'Lord, this tough spot you put me can't be a punishment from God, for Jesus had borne it on my behalf on the cross. There must be a greater purpose here'
When I face trouble	What have I done wrong to deserve this bad thing from God? What do I need to do to appease you?	I am sure God customized this hardship for me so I can grow more like Christ. He lived a much more righteous life than me, yet had to suffer

Christ has done it for me, perhaps I should do it for my team member once in a while.'

Table 4.1 shows the stark contrast between the likely outlook and attitudes that Damian and Grace show in terms of how they relate to their work and God as well as different areas of their lives.

Moralistic leaders will respond to God out of a sense of obligation and with the power of the flesh. That is not sustainable in the long run because that righteous obligation will crush them physically, emotionally, and spiritually. They will grow weary of doing better and more, turn into cynical and bitter individuals when failures and disappointment occur, and blame God for things that do not turn out the way they are. The moralistic individuals will never experience how the joy of the Lord becomes their true strength.

The gospel-centered leaders are completely different. The marvel of receiving what Christ has done for us on the cross compels us to perform with all our might for him in every single area of our lives. To perform with excellence is therefore a tangible fruit of the Gospel.

Indeed excellence is a Christian virtue because we serve an excellent God. The character of God is therefore the grounds of all human excellence. Everything God is and does is marked by excellence (Isaiah 44:6–8). He executed his plan to create the world so well that he was personally satisfied with the fruit of his labor. We pursue excellence because we were each created in God's image, and were called to reflect him (Matthew 5:48).

And while God could have chosen to sustain and manage this world on his own, he wants us to actively participate as his partners. We need to be vigilant how we build on the excellent foundation that he has put in place. Apostle Paul suggests that we ought to build with quality materials using the figures of gold, silver, and precious stones which are costly, imperishable, and permanent (1 Corinthians 3:12–15). What he referred to is in God's world; we need to ensure we give our best shot every day to produce the best possible product or service. It is not enough for Christian leaders to merely start each task with a prayer, or to avoid sinful practices in their daily work, but they need to excel in what they do in service to God and others.

Peter Drucker meets Saint Augustine

In one fine Spring morning, Peter Drucker and Saint Augustine had a rather serious chat over coffee in the city of God.

Drucker: 'The best way to predict your future is to create it.'
Augustine: 'You need to entrust your past to God's mercy, your present to His love, and your future to His providence.'
Drucker: 'Are you saying we should not work hard to determine our future?'
Augustine: 'Pray as though everything depended on God. Work as though everything depended on you.'
Drucker: 'Okay, in that case let me paraphrase: The best way to predict your future is to create it with all your might, and surrender it to God's might.'
Augustine: 'Hear, hear!'

Horizontal or vertical identity

This chapter helps Christian leaders to reflect on the basis of their identity. Those who look to their performance, instead of Christ, as the source of their identity will create their own performance treadmill and find themselves at the end of the day utterly exhausted and disappointed. Indeed our identity can only be derived either vertically or horizontally (Tripp, 2012, p. 22)

> Human beings are always assigning themselves some kind of identity. There are only two places to look. Either you will be getting your identity vertically, from who you are in Christ, or you will be shopping for it horizontally in the situations, experiences, and relationships of your daily life. This is true of everyone, but I am convinced that getting one's identity horizontally is a particular temptation for those in ministry.

As followers of Jesus, our identity is defined solely based on what Jesus accomplished through his humbling incarnation, his sinless life, his sin-atoning death, and his sin-conquering resurrection and ascension. In other words, our identity does not lie in what we have done, but in what Christ has done. Our identity is rooted securely in his Gospel.

We do not excel in our work to get accepted by God, but quite the contrary because we are accepted by God in Christ, we want to excel in our work for the sake of Christ. We are loved as we are in Christ not *because* of but *despite* our moral or technical performance for God.

I will conclude this chapter with a reflective prayer that I wrote many years ago for personal use. It has helped me over the years to get me back on track whenever my heart wanders away.

A morning prayer before work

Heavenly Father,
As I embark on my life routines and must-dos today,
help me not to forget that I am not my accomplishments,
that who I am is not defined by the quality of my works,
and the ensuing nods and praises that people give me.

Grant that the default mode of my heart
to prove myself, to please others, to perform even for you
is not dominating the way I approach my work today,
lest I worship the god of performance, yet again.

Plant my heart in deep in the liberating truth that
you love me because of who You are, not because of what I do.
My success or failure will never fluctuate that love,
For Christ died for me when I was still indifferent towards him.

Because of that same love, you do not leave me where I am,
change and shape my ransomed life in every way,
strengthening me to give my 110% at work today
through Christ and for his glory alone.

Notes

1 The comment is taken from an article on the Stanford Prison Experiment website entitled 'Philip Zimbardo's response to recent criticisms of the Stanford Prison Experiment'.

2 The comment is taken from a two-hour documentary produced by HBO entitled *Lady Gaga presents: Monster Ball tour at the Madison Square Garden*.

References

Anderson, H. J., Baur, J. E., Griffith, J. A., & Buckley, M. R. (2017). What works for you may not work for (Gen) Me: Limitations of present leadership theories for the new generation. *The Leadership Quarterly*, 28, 245–260.

Ashforth, B. E., Harrison, S. H., & Corley, K. G. (2008). Identification in organizations: An examination of four fundamental questions. *Journal of Management*, 34(3), 325–374.

Ashforth, B. E., & Mael, F. (1989). Social identity theory and the organization. *Academy of Management Review*, 14, 20–39.

Bankston, C., & Zhou, M. (2002). Being well vs. doing well: Self-esteem and school performance among immigrant and nonimmigrant racial and ethnic groups. *The International Migration Review*, 36(2), 389–415.

Costea, B., Watt, P., & Amiridis, K. (2015). What killed Moritz Erhardt? Internships and the cultural dangers of "positive" ideas. *TripleC*, 13(2), 379–380.

Day, E. (2013, October 5). Moritz Erhardt: The tragic death of a city intern. *The Guardian*. Accessed March 11, 2019.

Empson, L. (2017). *Leading professionals: Power, politics, and prima donnas*. New York, NY: Oxford.

Hewlett, S. A., & Carolyn, B. L. (2006). Extreme jobs: The dangerous allure of the 70-hour workweek. *Harvard Business Review*, 84(12), 49–59.

Immelt, J. (2015). GE's Jeff Immelt on digitizing in the industrial space. *McKinsey Quarterly*. Accessed March 11, 2019.

Kennedy, M. (2013, November 23). Bank intern Moritz Erhardt died from epileptic seizure, inquest told. *The Guardian*. Accessed March 11, 2019.

Malik, S. (2013, August 23). Moritz Erhardt intern death spurs bank of America Merrill Lynch review. *The Guardian*. Accessed March 11, 2019.

Nouwen, H. (1992). *Live of the beloved: Spiritual living in a secular world* (1st ed., pp. 32–36). New York: Crossroad.

Powlison, D. (1995). Idols of the heart and "vanity fair". *Journal of Biblical Counseling, 13*, 49.

Rogers, C. R. (1961). *On becoming a person: A psychotherapist's view of psychotherapy*. Houghton Mifflin.

Tripp, P. D. (2012). *Dangerous calling: Confronting the unique challenges of pastoral ministry* (p. 22). Crossway.

Zimbardo, P. (2007). *The Lucifer effect: Understanding how good people turn evil*. New York: Random House.

CHAPTER 5

When leaders live for people's approval

'If you live for people's acceptance, you'll die from their rejection.'
(*Lecrae Moore*)

Which one is worse, self-aggrandizing tyrants or people-pleasing clowns? This is a perennial question that has been entertained for years in classrooms and boardrooms. While both are certainly bad forms of leadership, the latter is easier to be camouflaged as a civilized and nuanced approach to leadership.

If I am seen as a leader who never tries to defend my position or decision (i.e., people-pleasers), I might be seen as a wise, mature, and easy-to-work-with leader. It is definitely a safer form of leadership to practice as it does not invite direct opposition. But the tendency to please people is equally deadly because it runs counter to the very definition of leadership.

At its essence, *leadership* implies a process of moving people from point A to B, in contrast to *management*, which refers to managing people at point A or point B. The journey to move people from point A to B requires the leader to influence, inspire, motivate them on the one hand, and direct, challenge, criticize them on the other hand. Leaders who have a preoccupation with obtaining the praise, acceptance, and approval of others will struggle to convince people to journey with them out of their comfort zone. What if they do not like it and resent the leaders as a result?

Think of the following scenario. As a team leader, the task of chairing meetings falls on you, but you agonize every time you ramble in a meeting in order to maintain that positive image about you. You come home from work feeling anxious about a remark you made to a potential key client. You know you should not be losing sleep over a little mistake that you are hardly responsible for, but you always do.

Instead of wondering what God, the most important being in the universe who made us and loves us, thinks about what we say and do, we are worried about what other people think of us. We might be eager to live for the approval of God, at least in theory, but in reality we live for the approval of others.

Consider the following questions: Whose approval matters most when you make major or even minor decisions in your lives? Whose approval do you crave when you prepare a presentation, help a colleague, solve a delicate problem, speak up for a cause, or lead an important meeting?

From fear of God to fear of people

The crowd was jubilant on that inaugural day of Israel's newly minted monarch, the first of its kind in the history of the nation. It was a time of turbulence and war in Israel, enemies from foreign nations were always looming large. King Saul was the answer of what the nation demanded to God through the aging prophet Samuel. Samuel was gobsmacked that the Israelites wanted to be like other nations, rather than fulfilling their calling to be distinctive among the nations on Earth. But what made the prophet completely dumbfounded was that God in his long-suffering mercy granted their request. That historic day circa 1040 BC when theocracy was replaced by monarchy was punctuated by a social commentary from God himself as he revealed to Samuel, 'They have not rejected you, but they have rejected me from being king over them' (1 Samuel 8:7).

The book of 1 Samuel notes Saul's humble beginning. The tall and handsome young man commenced his leadership career as a humble, God-fearing king. His first kingly act was to deal with the threat made by the Ammonites, and through his reliance on God brought a total victory for Israel. But his kingly reign was quickly spiralling down from that point onwards. When the Israelites were pinned down in a battle against the Philistines, Saul unlawfully offered burnt offerings to seek God's favor. His fear of the Philistines was bigger than his fear of God, who only authorized his prophet Samuel to offer sacrifices.

The second major blunder he made was his decision to spare the life of the king of the Amalekites in defiance of God's direct and clear command. Here is his attempt to justify himself in his own words to Samuel, 'I have sinned, for I have transgressed the commandment of the Lord and your words, because I feared the people and obeyed their voice' (1 Samuel 15:24). When a powerful ruler makes a bad decision driven by a desire to please people, we know that the end of his leadership is near. Note that Saul was not anxious about his enemies, he was anxious about being unpopular among his own people.

Even more telling was his next request, 'I have sinned; yet honor me now before the elders of my people and before Israel, and return with me, that I may bow before the Lord your God' (1 Samuel 15:30). Underlying that statement is an important leadership lesson rarely observed in leadership textbooks. Saul verbally confessed his sins, but his heart was miles away from his mouth. There was no remorse and repentance, as his main concern was really saving his face among his people. As history shows, Saul's obsession with what people think of him put his entire kingship and relationship with God in jeopardy. Here is the vital leadership lesson. An admission of guilt tempered by a last-ditch effort to save one's face is one sure way to end your leadership prematurely. Beggars can't be choosers.

Saul was subsequently overcome with envious fear towards David when God brought him into the picture as a potential successor. Towards the end of his leadership, Saul was yet again overwhelmed by his fear of people, this time of his old adversaries, the Philistine army. In a wilful disobedience to God who has given him multiple victories, he visited a medium to summon the spirit of the dead prophet Samuel for consultation.

The leadership of Saul serves as a cautionary tale for leaders everywhere that the most insidious problem of leadership is the fear of people. It has salient effects on the subtle, gradual decline of one's leadership. As Figure 5.1 depicts, Saul's leadership was

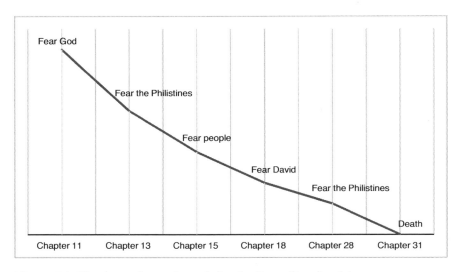

Figure 5.1 The fear of people and the decline of leadership

marked by downward movement from fear of God to fear of people.

Understanding fear of people

As illustrated in the leadership of Saul, fear of people represents the most ubiquitous yet least acknowledged leadership handicap (Welch, 1997). In the biblical sense, the phrase is contrasted to fear of God or reverence to God.

Fear of people refers to a spectrum of thoughts, emotions, and attitudes that we exhibit because we are being controlled by other people. Their opinions, assessments, judgements, approvals, or rejections have disproportionate effects on us. Our sense of self-worth is on a roller-coaster ride whenever we are being subjected to their biased views. What people say about something we do or do not do would animate our feeling for joy (or lack of it). The remote control of our emotional temperature is held by someone significant in our lives. Indeed attention, recognition, and praise of others often become cocaine for the ego, yet unlike other drugs, the users can still maintain their civility even when experiencing overdose.

In order to get a precise understanding of fear of people, it is worth thinking of other theoretically relevant but distinct concepts. For example, fear of people should be differentiated from a phobia known as *allodoxaphobia* (fear of hearing the opinions of others), which is a rare and irrational social phobia. People with this phobia avoid participating in events or activities that involves any sort of judgment. Since nearly every single area of work life does involve some assessment (e.g., performance review), people suffering from this phobia find it very debilitating to go to work. People who struggle with fear of people are different because instead of being anxious of hearing others' opinions, they live for other people's positive opinions. They crave for approval, acceptance, and praise.

Fear of people is also not identical to Fear of Missing Out (FOMO), a popular acronym commonly understood as a form of a compulsive anxiety that one might miss a rewarding opportunity that others are enjoying. It could be a social event, a novel experience, or a profitable investment. FOMO is exacerbated by addiction to social media, which gives us 24/7 access to what other people are doing. As Facebook and Instagram 'Likes' becomes an important gauge of approval, those who are not in-the-know with important events, experiences, or interactions will be seen as unpopular, ignored, or forgotten. They feel restless, wondering ceaselessly about something they could have possibly missed out that others are currently having.

Those with fear of people however do not have concern over the possibility of missing out on something per se, rather they want to ensure people think highly of them and that may mean consciously choosing to be out of touch with the latest social trend or experience. If FOMO is a pervasive apprehension to always stay connected, fear of people is a perpetual desire for approval regardless of whether one stay connected or disconnected.

Granted Christian leaders are not immune from fear of people. What makes matters worse is that rather than admitting that they have the fear, an overwhelming majority dress it up in the more politically correct and socially acceptable façade of stress. It is much more elegant to say 'I am stressed out but that is the price of leadership' rather than admitting 'I always feel the need to fulfil what people expect of me.'

Inordinate fear

In order to have a proper grasp of fear of people, it is critical to understand that the opposite of fear of people is not a complete disregard of what people think of us. Leaders who have no empathic response to what people say would by definition turn into psychopaths. The opposite of fear of people is paying attention to others' opinions without being controlled by it. Why is it important to be aware of this?

Because leaders need to listen not just selectively but attentively to the opinion of others to understand their needs, struggles, hopes, and aspirations. More importantly, leaders need to have inputs and feedback from others in order to stay accountable. But there is a clear line between listening well to and cowering silently at their comments.

As such, the real culprit here is not the opinion or approval of others per se, but its inordinate influence on us. If we base our self-worth on the love, acceptance, attention, praise from someone, that individual owns something substantial that can be used against us. We are anxious because they have the capacity to embarrass us, disappoint us, reject us, betray us, lie to us, or even attack us. Because we allow them to strike fear within our hearts, we give them the rights to regulate what we feel, think, and do. We see them in a disproportionate size. They are bigger than God.

A self-diagnosis

How do you know that as a leader, you are being controlled by what other people think of you? The following list of reflective questions might help you diagnose in which area we let other ourselves be influenced too significantly by others. It includes manifestations of fear of people in the literature such as peer pressure and codependency, which have been studied empirically. These questions provide hints to help you identify the idol of approval that lurk behind. There might be other pertinent hints, but these ones particularly speak to leaders. These questions will be most useful when they are used in the presence of others who know you inside out – colleagues, team members, or your spouse. Given the prevalence of self-response bias, their inputs will be invaluable to assess the extent to which one lives for the approval of others.

1 Do you often feel pressured to meet the expectations of others?

2 Do you strive for excellence primarily to create the impression that you are better than others?

3 Do you find it challenging to say no to people's requests?

4 Do you overtly or covertly demand respect from people at work?

5 Do you feel compelled to help people solve their problems?

6 Do you feel worried whether people like or dislike you?

7 Do you easily get offended by what people say about you?

8 Do you struggle making difficult decisions given the potential negative consequences if things go wrong?

9 Do you consciously make every single effort to minimize the possibility of embarrassing yourself?

10 Do you engage in white lies to project a positive image about yourself?

11 Do you secretly envy those who are more successful than you are?

12 Do you get irritated easily?

13 Do you tend to avoid certain individuals?

14 Do you bribe and beg to mend a rupture in a relationship?

15 Do you disdain those who do not respect you?

16 Do you often feel unappreciated?

17 Do you speak up when someone keeps undermining you?

18 Would you rather stay silent rather than gently confronting people?

19 Do you apologize often and unnecessarily for the things you say or do?

20 Do you find it hard to ask for help?

21 Do you struggle to admit your mistake and apologize?

22 Do you confess your sins to others?

23 Do you have worries that your life might be exposed?

24 Are you constantly wondering in conversations what the other person is thinking?

25 Do you always suspect someone is judging you or laughing at you?

26 Are you reluctant to share your accomplishments to avoid sounding like bragging?

27 Are you a social chameleon, changing yourself to fit the surrounding crowd?

28 Do you act one way when you are at work, and another way when at home or church?

Fear of people and their effects on followers

Fear of people significantly affects the way leaders relate to other people, including their team members. The late leadership author John Gardner famously quipped 'Pity the leaders caught between *unloving critics* and *uncritical lovers*' (Gardner, 1990, p. 135).

Some team members are *unloving critics*; they make it an important part of their life mission to criticize their leader in every single decision the leader makes or does not make. They do it not because they want to arrive at the best decision, but because they draw energy from becoming a self-appointed opposition to the leader. What they do is suck the emotional energy of the leaders dry. *Unloving critics* are identical to the theorizing of alienated followers, those who are independent and critical in their thinking but passive in carrying out their role (Kelley, 1988).

On the other end of the spectrum are *uncritical lovers*, individuals who rely on flattery and ingratiation tactics to accelerate their agenda. They are yes-people, sycophants who acquiesce to every wish and whim of the leader. Their admiration for the leader erodes their capacity to objectively assess the leader's decisions and actions (or lack of them).

When faced with the option of gathering around them *unloving critics* or *uncritical lovers*, most leaders prefer the latter. This is particularly true for those leaders with fragile egos. *Unloving critics* are often systematically ignored and ostracized by leaders who feel annoyed or insulted by their attitudes. In fact, many of them get fired. Conversely, leaders like to be surrounded by *uncritical lovers* because they feed leaders with a false sense of security. They often become the source of the leader's intellectual and emotional energy. Things get done when leaders work with them given their constant, reliable support.

However, *uncritical lovers* pose an equal, if not bigger, danger to the leader. The oft-quoted observation of psychiatrist Norman Vincent Peale is right on the money here: 'The trouble with most of us is that we are rather ruined by praise than loved by criticism.' While the overwhelming majority of leaders might prefer sycophants rather than dissenters, given enough time they both will render leaders ineffective.

Unloving critics, despite their hurtful methods, might give criticism that is wholly or partially true, while *uncritical lovers* only convey things that are pleasant to the ears. The comparison between the two groups are highlighted in the following remark (Bennis, 1994, p. xxii).

> Nothing will sink a leader faster than surrounding him- or herself with yes-men and women. Even when principled nay-sayers are wrong, they force leaders to re-evaluate their positions and to poke and prod their assumptions for weaknesses. Good ideas are only made stronger by being challenged.

Scholars have suggested that leaders should turn both groups into *loving critics*, those who care deeply enough to give honest feedback to the leaders. My recommendation is slightly different, instead of empowering followers to be *loving critics*, a wise leader should aim for *critical lovers*.

Critical lovers are followers who sincerely love their leader, willing to speak the truth to their leader out of and in that love. They genuinely support the leader because they know that it is God who called the leader to provide direction and guidance to the people. They respect, encourage, and support the leader in his or her leadership role. Yet it is that same love that compel them to confront their leaders gently but firmly when they see the leaders start to deviate from God's ways.

■ The solutions to fear of people

I am mindful of the fact that by virtue of their position, leaders are always tempted to pay too much attention to what their subordinates, superiors, colleagues, and clients say about them. There is a reason why the 360-degree evaluation is very popular as a feedback tool. How do you then deal with the judgement and opinions of people?

The apostle Paul experienced a similar sort of conundrum around living for approval when he was ministering to the churches in the city of Corinth. It is in this city of Corinth that he went through an ordeal as a church planter and spiritual leader of the many congregations he served. The reason why Paul felt that he was being judged by the Corinthians was because the Corinthians had a deep ambivalence towards the ministry of Paul as an apostle of Jesus Christ.

The Corinth church was eating itself alive from inside with the pervasiveness of personality cults within the congregations. Conflicts and dissension among church members were common as people grouped themselves around their allegiance to different leaders, much to the dismay of the leaders themselves. They claimed to be the fan club members of Paul the church founder, Apollos the charismatic teacher, Cephas the Jewish hero, or Jesus himself the non-bloc figure (or so they thought).

Paul was also being consistently compared to the false teachers that were misleading the people of God in Corinth. When he received some financial assistance from select congregations he served (which was a common practice for itinerant preachers at the time), they would accuse Paul of some ulterior motive. However, when Paul declined it from other congregations, they would label Paul as an arrogant minister who undermined the token of love shown by the people he served. He found himself in a Catch-22 situation.

Against that challenging terrain of ministry, Paul refused to let his life to be unfairly judged by the Corinthians. What he wrote to the Corinthians contain invaluable leadership lessons most relevant for contemporary Christian leaders who struggle with the tendency to please others. Paul wrote to them, 'But with me it is a very small thing that I should be judged by you or by any human court. In fact, I do not even judge myself. For I am not aware of anything against myself, but I am not thereby acquitted' (1 Corinthians 4:3–4). There are at least four recommendations that leaders can employ to deal with fear of people:

1. Refuse to be trapped in the courtroom of people's opinion

Leaders by virtue of their positions know intimately that it is easy to base their sense of self on what people say and think about their decisions and actions. If we give people the permission to judge our worth, our lives are always in a state of constant flux depending on whether we receive blessings or curses. That is why Paul brought the courtroom metaphor into his argument. We cannot help feeling we are on trial daily if the opinions of people loom large, regardless whether they are positive or negative.

Praise and criticism are legitimate as long as we don't allow these twin brothers to put our joy on a roller coaster ride. If your identity is not rooted in something or someone much bigger than the most important people of your life, both their criticisms and praises will have the same devastating effects on you. Criticism is usually treated as the evil twin brother. No doubt criticisms will send you into a dwindling spiral of feeling unworthy. We have our own defense attorney within our hearts who will leap into action and say to us, 'Don't listen to him. Who does he think he is to treat you like that? You are nothing like what he just described!'

But praises are equally deadly, though the effect is not immediate. You will be elated at first, but soon after, you will be crippled with anxiety. What if I cannot live up to those praiseworthy expectations? What if I lose my charm and genius? What if I have a lapse of judgment or make a terrible blunder? For the insecure, praises are just the slower version of criticism. It is important therefore to learn from Paul to stay out of the courtroom for good, no longer being controlled by what people think or say about him.

2. Discern the influential voices in our hearts

The secular contemporary approach to psychology is absolutely spot on about one thing: The most influential person in your life is *you*. We tend to think that the most influential person in our lives is our significant others (spouse, parents, boss, or colleagues). Yet, no one in the world has more significant effects on you than you.

No matter how deep you think your direct supervisor at work has shaped the way you think and feel, your supervisor's influence will have no effect unless you give permission to yourself to absorb that influence and say to yourself, 'She is right, I need to toughen up' or 'It turns out it's ok for people to cut corners in this company, I too should be more "creative" next time.' The opinions of others have impact on our lives only because we allow them to by affirming or disaffirming them. No one in this God's green earth is more influential to you than you.

While we hold the control of who and what can or cannot influence us, often we are not aware of the many voices around us that try to take control of our life priorities, decisions, and attitudes. At the very least, we are not constantly aware of the voices that relentlessly aim to shape our lives. If we look at them from a biblical worldview, we will find that there is more at stake that just mere opinions.

From the very beginning in the pre-fall story of mankind in the book of Genesis, we were told that there were two voices that influenced Adam and Eve, the voice of God and the voice of the serpent. The serpent was mentioned in the first book of the Bible as 'the craftiest of the beasts in the field,' which was also made by God (Genesis 3:1) and referred to in the last book of the Bible as 'the devil and Satan, the deceiver of the whole world' (Revelation 12:9).

God then said to Adam that his failure was that he listened to the voice of his wife (Genesis 3:17), who had been undoubtedly influenced by Satan himself. As such, behind Eve's opinion is the influence of Satan, who aims to get the first couple to doubt God, overthrow his good and gracious rule, and become like God.

Living in our fallen nature in the fallen world means there are influences of the devil, the world, and our sinful flesh that are at work on a daily basis. They might masquerade themselves in various forms such as the well-meaning exhortation of our parents, pep talks given by our coaches, tough love expressed by our mentors, or kind words of encouragement of our friends. Left unchecked, they always put us back into the courtroom of opinions. These are perhaps some of the more familiar examples:

'Prove to him you're worth something'
'Prove you have important contributions to make'

'Show others that you are relevant'

'Make sure others see what you have sacrificed'

'Don't let him treat you like that'

'Of course, you don't deserve that tone'

'Seriously, you are better than that person in many different ways'

'You deserve an apology from that person, make sure she knows that'

'It is only fair if you demand some respect from that person'

'Who does he think he is to quip me with that question!'

These voices often speak so loudly it creates a deafening silence that numbs our affection for God. What makes these voices very subtle is that they creep up not just once in a blue moon, but perhaps fifty times a day in our seemingly insignificant routines and interactions we have with various people: Our boss and colleagues, spouse, parents, siblings, friends. If we allow these voices to reign supreme in our hearts, we soon become our own lord. No wonder conversations at work or home often turn sour in no time. Even relationships with others at the church can feel like a juggling performance on a tightrope. We need to turn down its volume, sometimes quite considerably.

3. Be mindful of biased perception of self

As mentioned previously, there exists an ever-present influence of the devil, the world, and our sinful flesh through the opinions of others. Yet, we often do not realize that they are more lethal than we think. It is indeed wise to play down the significance of the opinions of others, but it does not mean that we should subsequently go to the other extreme for we will be sent right back playing into the hands of the evil one.

To put it differently, our attempts to minimize the opinion of others often propel us to exalt our own. 'Who cares about what other people think or what the world thinks, the only opinion that matters is mine!' Engaging in this sort of self-talk to counteract negative opinions and build self-confidence or self-esteem is akin to getting out of the frying pan into the fire.

Contemporary psychology tells us that people have a low self-esteem problem because they have a low opinion of themselves. The solution therefore is to ignore the opinion of others, and focus solely on one opinion that does and should truly count, namely our own. For example, we need to deal with the voice of others that says, 'You will never deserve to be promoted' by convincing yourself using the following self-talk 'You are more than capable. You can do anything you put your mind to. Prove them wrong!'

By the grace of God, apostle Paul was fully aware of the double-bind situation he was in. After telling us that other people's opinion means very little to him, he said in the same breath, 'In fact, I do not even judge myself. For I am not aware of anything against myself, but I am not thereby acquitted' (1 Corinthians 4:3–4). Here is a most helpful paraphrase of Paul's sentence, 'I don't care what you think – but I don't care what *I* think. I have a very low opinion of your opinion of me – but I have a very low opinion of *my* opinion of me' (Keller, 2012, p. 26).

It does not mean that Paul goes around telling people that he is a nobody. What he meant by not judging himself is he did not pay attention even to his own opinion about himself. Note that boasting to others that we are somebody or nobody is both a sign of self-obsessed personality.

On the contrary, drawing on the work of C.S. Lewis, Keller argued that to be truly free of one's own judgement is a sign of gospel humility. 'Because the essence of gospel-humility is not thinking more of myself or thinking less of myself, it is thinking of myself less. Gospel-humility is not needing to think about myself' (Keller, 2012, pp. 31–32).

Practically speaking, Paul implies that others' assessment and self-assessment cannot be relied upon, for the outcome of both assessments 'may depress beyond reason or exalt beyond measure' (Morris, 2008, p. 73). Both inspection and introspection are futile to produce an objective and true sense of who one is. This admission is not a small feat for someone of Paul's stature. From his writings, we knew that he was a highly educated, influential, and effective leader of the church. Yet he was humble enough to say that he was not infallible, and that awareness made him impossible to trust his own view about himself.

The fact that Paul has a clear conscience makes no difference. In the New International Version, 1 Corinthians 4:4 reads, 'My conscience is clear, but that does not make me innocent.' His conscience may be clear – but he knows that even if he does have a clear conscience, that does not necessarily mean he is innocent. Hitler might have had a clear conscience, but it did not mean he was innocent. His conscience did not and cannot justify him.

In summary, Paul did not ignore the critical and unfair evaluation that people have only to replace it with his own standard. In the midst of harsh words and judgmental attitude, he did not resort to a self-pity and self-justifying mode. When he wrote that he did not even judge himself, what he meant was *self* cannot be trusted.

In our modern vernacular, we call this tendency to view ourselves in an elevated manner as self-response bias. But the antidote of low self-esteem is not high self-esteem. Contrary to countless books on strategies to boost self-esteem, the doctrine of indwelling sin tells us that the most basic problem with human beings lies in the sinful self within. Self is never the key to the solution to low self-esteem precisely because self is the root of the problem.

4. Turn to Christ whose opinion really matters

How can we ignore the opinions of others without turning us into larger-than-life individuals in our own heads? How did Paul manage to minimize the effect of people's judgement on himself without feeling like he was the supreme judge? The Gospel provides the answer.

Following his decommercialization act of the temple on the Monday of Passion Week, Jesus encountered on Tuesday premeditated, malicious entrapments. Politically-charged questions were asked by the corrupt leaders who for years have been plotting against him. The right-wing Pharisees wanted to get rid of Jesus because of his theological views. But they knew the Roman military won't arrest Jesus because of mere theology. They needed to make Jesus a political threat for the Romans. For that reason, they colluded with the left-wing Herodians to trap Jesus. After all, the enemy of my enemy is my friend.

The chain of events put in motion by the unholy alliance in the lead-up to the arrest of Jesus and its ensuing kangaroo trial was so intense it makes the plots against Ethan Hunt or Jason Bourne feel like ho-hum affairs. Executed with surgical precision during the Passover in Jerusalem were tactics such as flattery (Mark 12:13), spying (Luke 20:20), perjury (Luke 23:2), and paying a snitch (Luke 24:3–4). Little did they know that the very man they spent so much time plotting against to kill was the man whose sole purpose to come to the world was to die for his enemies.

That's the essence of Christianity: A man who died for his enemies. He bore the just punishment of God upon the sins of those who ignored, mocked, and rebelled against the Creator God. That was the reason why Jesus Christ went on trial without complaining despite it being clearly a kangaroo court. He faced an unjust trial on our behalf without complaining so that we never have to face any trial of unfair human opinions.

We need to turn our eyes upon Jesus Christ, our God-Man, who years earlier before facing the unjust trial was tempted in the wilderness by the devil with the same judgmental voice: 'Prove you are the beloved. Change these stones into bread. Be sure you're famous. Jump from the temple, and you will be known.' In reply, Jesus essentially said, 'No, I don't have to prove anything. I am already the beloved.' He did not need approval and acceptance of people because he had already been approved by his heavenly father, who previously declared during his baptism, 'This is my beloved Son, with whom I am well pleased' (Matthew 3:17).

As explained in the previous chapter, that declaration is also ours by virtue of our union with Christ. In Christ, we too have been approved and accepted by God. We don't need to prove anything or do anything to have a secure sense of self. It's all done once-and-for-all by the finished work of Christ at the cross. In Christ, we are empowered to say 'Ssshh!' whenever that nagging voice comes up whether it is three or fifty times a day. As the volume of those voices is turned down, we can then preach the Gospel to ourselves in the stillness of our souls.

In doing so, we turn our attention to someone who is mightier than anything or anyone found within the realm of creation, and cares for you deeply enough to shrink into the realm of creation to care for us. We need both, for one is insufficient to capture our attention. We tend to ignore those in authority who do not genuinely care towards us. We tend to take for granted those who genuinely care about us but are not powerful enough to warrant our attention and affection.

Only Jesus Christ fits those two criteria in the truest sense of the word. He has all authority in heaven and on earth, yet loves us to the end by laying down his life for us. Jesus did not decide to die for us because we are worthy. It is precisely the opposite. Jesus died for us the unworthy to make us worthy.

If he, by whom, through whom, and for whom all things visible and invisible were created, had died for us while we were still his enemies, we would forever stand on a solid ground for our acceptance. Criticism and rejection from people will not erode it. Approval from others will be much less significant for us, and have its proper place without turning us into approval-junkies. It has been well said that 'Jesus Christ knows the worst about you, nevertheless he is the one who loves you most' (Tozer, 2009, p. 129). That is the good news of the Gospel.

The Gospel therefore enables us to live for the audience of One. We will stop keeping score in life to know we count because we now know that we always count before God. In a typical Puritan fashion, Richard Baxter (1691) outlines in his classic work rational arguments in support of the view that it makes more sense to live for God's approval rather than for people's approval. Here are seven reasons that are more readily applicable to leaders.

The advantages of pleasing God rather than people

1 You have but one to please instead of multitudes; and a multitude of masters are harder pleased than one.
2 And it is one that put upon you nothing that is unreasonable, for quantity or quality.
3 And one that is perfectly wise and good, not liable to misunderstand your case and actions.
4 And he is one that is impartial and most just, and is no respecter of persons (cf. Acts 10:34).

5 And he is one that is a competent judge, that hath fitness and authority, and is acquainted with your hearts, and every circumstance and reason of your actions.

6 And he is one that is constant and unchangeable; and is not pleased with one thing today, and another contrary tomorrow; nor with one person this year, whom he will be weary of the next.

7 He is one that will not be moved by tale-bearers, whisperers, or false accusers, nor can be perverted by any misinformation.

Do people's opinions matter? The double-edge effect of the gospel

The foregoing sections tell us that in order to stop living for people's approval, we cannot rely on the secular solution that says, 'Ignore what people say about you. Love yourself!' without getting into a greater danger of self-worship.

The religious version of this is equally lethal where we use God to feed into our sense of self-importance, 'Ignore what people say about you. God loves you more than he loves them or anyone for that matter!'

The Gospel is entirely different. We realize that we are no better than our harshest critics because we stand equally condemned for our sins before the just and holy judgement of God, but Christ was condemned on our behalf instead. The Gospel says, 'Ignore what people say about you. Ignore what you say about you. Because the only person whose opinion counts, Jesus Christ, took the punishment of sins that both you and everyone else deserve.'

Let me take you one step further to understand the double-edge effect of the Gospel. The Gospel is a game-changer for Christian leaders because it turns us from people-pleasers to people-lovers. The same Gospel that makes people's approval, praise, and acceptance no longer matter for us also makes us seek people's approval, praise, and acceptance.

Because of the Gospel, their opinions *do not* matter, yet for the sake of the Gospel, their opinions *do* matter.

Table 5.1 Paul's paradox around pleasing people in Galatia and Corinth

A Servant of Christ	A Servant to All
So what now: Am I looking for human likes or God's likes? Do I try to please humans? If I still want to try to please humans, then I am not a servant of Christ (Galatians 1:10).	Enslave yourselves to one another through active love (Galatians 5:13)
You were bought with a price; do not become bondservants of men (1 Corinthians 7:23)	For though I am free from all, I have made myself a servant to all, that I might win more of them (1 Corinthians 9:19).

This principle is beautifully illustrated in the attitudes exemplified by the apostle Paul when as a church planter and leader, he had to deal with difficult people of all stripes. The following table shows the contrast between his exhortations he gave to the people he led in Galatia and Corinth.

Imagine writing a two-page letter where on the first page you say one thing, and on the next you say the exact opposite. How could he contradict himself in a short space of time, twice? One might be tempted to construe him as a chameleon leader who adapts at will for political expediency or a Machiavellian leader who says whatever needs to be said to fulfil his ambition. But there is a better explanation.

On the one hand, he was saying that he was not willing to compromise his leadership by acquiescing to certain powerful individuals at the church. Paul knew too well that every leader who leads others for a great cause would expect critics and opponents. There are diverse groups with vested interests and hidden agenda. While Paul is not a person who was rigid or lacking negotiation skills, he would never let other people control him, for he was performing only to the audience of One. That was why he wrote quite bluntly to the Galatians that if he was still trying to please humans, he could never be called a servant of Christ.

On the other hand, Paul wrote that he was readily available to become a servant to all. Was he a servant of Christ or a servant to all? He seemed to be both, simultaneously. This paradoxical stance needs further elaboration. In an emotionally-charged response to his ungrateful critics at Corinth who challenged the authenticity of his ministry, Paul outlined his personal rights to be appreciated as an apostle of Jesus Christ, to be financially supported, to have a spouse who should also be financially supported, and to be freed from working for a living so he can devote his time exclusively for the Gospel ministry (1 Corinthians 9:1–6).

He then gave multiple compelling reasons from the Scripture and common sense in support of those rights that forever silenced his critics who should have known better (1 Corinthians 9:7–14). In a nutshell Paul essentially exclaimed, 'C'mon Corinthians, use your common sense, read your Scripture, be fair, know your religious tradition, and remember Christ's command. And you will know that I don't pluck these rights out of thin air!'

However, Paul did not stop there, for the whole point of airing his rights in public was to set an example for others that he did not cling to any of those rights, let alone demanding others to fulfil them to the fullest extent. Instead he willingly surrendered each and every one of those rights to Christ and voluntarily endure anything as a consequence. His motive was crystal clear: He did not want those rights to be 'an obstacle in the way of the gospel of Christ' (1 Corinthians 9:12b).

As believers, we have been freed from sin, hell, death, the devil, the wrath of God in and through Christ and him alone. But our freedom is not a license to do whatever we want or an opportunity to demand our rights. To be sure, we tend to view freedom as the rights to do whatever we like. Ask a five-year-old or a teenager (even a full-grown person for that matter), chances are they will concur with that view.

But those who associate freedom with having a sense of entitlement to have their personal rights met are actually not free at all. They are prisoners of their hearts' inclination to demand things to be done when and how they want them. The preoccupation with a burgeoning sense of entitlement is one of the greatest problems in our generation today.

The prevalent attitude can be summarized as follows: 'As long as I do not violate other people's rights, I have the right to demand my RIGHTS!' The slightest hints of unappreciated or violated rights will make one run amok with sinful anger, disdain, and self-pity almost instantaneously. Christian leaders who are more conscious of their rights rather than responsibilities will struggle to be effective for the kingdom's work. It is not uncommon to hear churches split because the leaders insist on demanding their rights.

The apostle Paul, who was an upstanding, religious, and highly educated Roman citizen summarized his life in the following sentences: 'I have made myself a servant to all, that I might win more.' Centuries later Martin Luther echoed Paul when he wrote, 'A Christian man is a most free lord of all, subject to none. A Christian man is a most dutiful servant of all, subject to all.'

History has since noted that the most effective strategy in missional living is renouncing our personal rights to Christ. Paul instinctively knew that he was free to exercise his rights, but in order to win as many people to Christ, he accommodated others with sacrificial love in cultural areas without compromising himself in moral and doctrinal areas.

His message to Corinthians was loud and clear when it comes to moral precepts (e.g., 'Flee from sexual immorality') and doctrinal teaching (e.g., the resurrection of the body). No second guessing with these absolute moral and doctrinal issues.

But when it comes to cultural issues, he was very flexible. He went to a great length explaining when it was appropriate and inappropriate to, for example, eat food that has been offered to idol worship or adhere to the Jewish law of circumcision in the case of Timothy and Titus. At face value he may appear like a chameleon, but a closer examination would reveal that he was very consistent with his deep conviction. That is, to win as many people to Christ as humanly possible, he would be all things to all people in non-moral areas.

In other words, although Paul had every right not to be bound by other people's requests and demands, he voluntarily abandoned those rights and chose to be a servant for others in order to bring them to Christ. This does not imply that Christian leaders should be completely stripped of their unalienable rights (e.g., liberty, life). It does imply however that Christian leaders should be willing *not* to demand the rights they deserve (e.g., the right to be respected or appreciated, the right to be heard, the right to compensated, the right to get what their counterparts enjoy).

How can Paul (and by extension, we) possibly do that, pleasing other people by becoming all things to them? Every cell in our body will scream against the idea of foregoing our rights. We will never be able to do it until we truly grasp that Jesus Christ had become all things to us and for us. 'Though he was in the form of God . . . [he] made himself nothing, taking a form of a servant, being born in the likeness of men. And being found in human form, he humbled himself by becoming obedient to the point of death, even death on the cross' (Philippians 2:6–8).

The degree to which that truth permeates our heart will determine our willingness to please other people because of Christ. He lived a sacrificial life not so that we are exempted from it, but for the very purpose that when we live sacrificially we become like him.

In summary, being a servant to Christ and a servant to all are not contradictory. The distinguishing factor is the motivation of the heart underlying that leadership outlook.

The Gospel tells us that we no longer need to live for people's approval because Christ, the one whose approval really counts, has fully and eternally received us on the cross when we were still his enemies. Yet, the Gospel also tells us that we should live for people's approval for the sake of Christ, who took the form of a servant to stoop so low to our level in order to reach us. Christian leaders must attempt to please people not to gain praise, popularity, votes, but to be able to serve them more effectively and efficiently.

Because of the Gospel, their opinions *do not* matter, and for the sake of the Gospel their opinions *do* matter.

Four implications for gospel-centered leaders

Christian leaders who are people-pleasers will always be controlled by people's opinions. Thankfully, the Gospel liberates them to become people-lovers, those who are no longer swayed by people's opinions regardless of whether they are sincere or insecure, accurate or inaccurate. Yet they simultaneously pay full attention to people's individual opinions (and needs, struggles, aspirations) in order to serve them well. Such leaders put the Gospel as the center of the many facets of their leadership roles.

	Positive	
Passive	Receive compliments without pride	Affirm others in earnest
	Take criticism without bitterness	Speak the truth in love
	Negative	Active

Figure 5.2 Gospel-centered leaders and people's approval

There are at least four implications for the Gospel-centered leaders when it comes to dealing with the approval of others. The implications are organized into the following quadrants in the passive-active and negative-positive areas.

Receive compliments without pride

By virtue of their position, leaders are simultaneously blessed and cursed with many compliments they receive from people they lead. They are blessed because they have confirmation that what they say and do make positive differences in the lives of others. They are cursed because compliments left unchecked might lead them into the treacherous road of perdition. Leaders would be wise to remember that 'Compliments are like perfume: ok to sniff, but deadly to drink.'[1]

We should be appreciative of every genuine compliment we receive, and showing it by verbally and sincerely thanking the givers. At times it might be proper to probe further in what specific ways your speech or actions have been helpful to them. However, we should remember to quickly deflect this compliment to the source of all things good, God himself, knowing that pride is crouching at the door, eager to control us.

The following verse is perhaps the single most important reminder that will come in handy whenever someone gives us a compliment: 'What do you have that you did not receive? If then you received it, why do you boast as if you did not receive it?' (1 Corinthians 4:7).

How do we know that we have truly grasped the Gospel when it comes to receiving compliments? By observing our knee-jerk response to the absence of a compliment following a job well done.

In fact, as leaders operate in a transient culture where people are increasingly fickle in their loyalties and affections, it is quite probable to encounter a scenario when the person who once gave us very positive compliments is speaking ill of us behind our back or to our face.

Our longing for constant praise and recognition from others means that we have not really tried to plumb the depths of what Christ has amply and generously given us. Holding the Gospel truth will prevent us from being a compliment addict. Christ has fully accepted us when he died for us on the cross, and that is more than sufficient. No amount of people's acceptance will inflate our true joy, and no amount of people's rejection can deflate it.

Affirm others in earnest

Since their identity is secured in Christ, gospel-centered leaders are not afraid of being outshined by more intelligent and talented followers or colleagues. As such, they have no difficulties verbally and genuinely appreciating others' efforts, strengths, and abilities. They will seize the opportunities to recognize someone's excellence in front of their colleagues, if and when it is appropriate to do so. They do not engage in public recognition as a means to shame or motivate others to up their game, but to highlight the specific contributions of the person receiving the praise.

Research shows that humble leaders who make it their habits to affirm and praise followers' strengths and compliment their contributions will enhance follower engagement and psychological freedom (Owens & Hekman, 2012). It does not then imply that they are turning a blind eye on the followers' areas of incompetence, rather they are more attuned to their unique strengths and efforts.

They are quick to spot their positive rather than negative aspects of the followers' contributions. This leadership capacity has a positive side effect. Followers are more receptive to their leaders' negative feedback if they feel that their strengths and contributions are always recognized.

Sincerity is the important operative word in the context of praising others, a lack thereof might be a signal of a lack of understanding of the Gospel. If we give insincere compliments to flatter people in order to obtain their approval or respect, we are essentially expecting from others what only Christ can give us in full.

While genuine praise is key, what makes a compliment Gospel-centered is when we give compliments not for our or their vain glory, but for the God's glory (Crabtree, 2011). That is, we applaud people for doing something excellent in the strength and wisdom God supplies them ('The way you handled that difficult conflict was really commendable, you have showed what one can do when one relies fully on Christ'). In doing so, we do not just acknowledge the God who began and is continuing a good work in the recipient of our praise, but also anticipate the future praise that God himself will give to his faithful servants, 'Well done, good and faithful servant.'

Ask yourself how many times a day you verbally affirm the strengths and efforts of others who work with you. In order to show our genuine interest in the person, we compliment others; there are a few practical things we can do. First, be specific. Saying 'Great job!' is quite vague and dubious. It is much more helpful to specify, for example, how the evidence-based rationale in section C she put together and argued winsomely has convinced the client of the merit of the project. A specific acknowledgement of one's initiative, effort, tenacity, enthusiasm, attention to details, or achievement ensures that the recipient will not confuse our praise with polite mannerism.

Second, we can end our compliments with a probing question (e.g., 'What you did in that project was out of the ordinary, how did you do it?'). Better yet, engage the recipient in a follow-up task or project that involves her employing the skill that she did well. These simple tips help the recipient to better understand why they deserve the compliment and encourage them to further develop that particular strength.

Take criticism without bitterness

Criticism is the flip side of compliments, and no leaders can escape it. However else you define the leader-follower relationship at work or church, at its core it is about sinners with glorified titles serving other sinners. As such, leaders should always begin their leadership roles on the assumption that leadership comes with the occupational hazard of receiving criticism.

Broadly speaking there are two categories of criticism based on the intent with which it is given, constructive and destructive. Constructive criticism is generally given with the intent of improved performance in the context of 360-degree feedback interventions. Destructive criticism typically involves an unfavorable opinion concerning the leader with the intent that the leader will change his or her position or behavior.

Research tells us that there are a number of ways leaders can respond to criticism (Eubanks et al., 2010):

1   Ambiguity or vagueness, which is a strategy to save face in response to a difficult or awkward situation,

2   Verbal aggression, which includes an attack on one's character or competence,

3   Deception, which produces false impressions and inaccurate conclusions,

4   Avoidance, which typically leads to more intensified conflicts, and

5   Collaboration, which has been thought to yield more positive outcomes.

It is useful to think through these approaches to raise our awareness; however it is merely a toolbox that cannot and will not empower us to change our approach to handle criticism. Leaders need something more powerful than a toolbox.

The Gospel functions as an ultimate buffer for leaders when it comes to dealing with criticism. Psychologists often talk about a buffering effect whereby a psychosocial resource like social support softens the impact of negative life events on one's well-being. The Gospel is an ultimate buffer because the social support that one gets comes from Christ Jesus, the King of kings and Lord of lords. Given the bitterness-buffering effect of the Gospel, leaders are empowered to in fact handle criticism more gracefully and proactively.

Specifically, they will be more willing to foster a conducive culture where followers are in fact encouraged to give constructive criticism to the leader. Rather than passively waiting for criticism, they should actively solicit them. Being fully aware of followers' reluctance of providing negative feedback for fear of the consequences, leaders should give their followers the right to question the actions and decisions preferably before they are executed or implemented. They need to give their followers verbal permissions on numerous occasions to catch a glimpse of a character flaw or lapse in judgement.

Being in an accountability relationship is a crucial safeguard for leaders primarily because leaders are prone to self-deception, perhaps more so than average human beings given the elitist culture, status, and prestige often associated with leadership positions. Given *the remnants* of *indwelling sin*, we are often blind to our own weaknesses.

Even worse, our capacity to deceive ourselves is much greater than our capacity to deceive others. We are quite adept at identifying self-deception in others. We can detect if someone tried to rationalize their socially unacceptable behaviors, but recognizing the same things in our own hearts is much more difficult and cumbersome. Followers' criticism helps leaders to realize their blind spots, keep their ego in check, and their edge sharp. It might actually be the very thing that prevents something destructive from happening to the leader and/or the organization.

Leaders with fear of people would struggle having an accountability relationship with their direct reports. Many leaders say to their followers, 'Do tell me if there are things that I did wrong but didn't realize.' But the minute someone does that, they get offended, become defensive, and seek to retaliate.

German philosopher Friedrich Nietzsche was only half-right when he wrote, 'That which does not kills us, makes us stronger.' Criticisms might make us more thick-skinned and resilient to face the next leadership challenge, yet it would simultaneously make us more cynical, bitter, and calculative. One's unkind words that grow into disappointment and bitterness will make us more cautious and suspicious of others, caring about them less, loving them less.

Criticism for leaders might be a clear and present affliction, but the Gospel is a clear and present comfort. The Gospel comforts us by presenting the right perspective we should have – in light of what Jesus experienced on the cross, our annoyance suddenly feels like an awful pity party gone wrong. On the other hand, the Gospel empowers you to speak the truth in love to that person.

Speak the truth in love

Christian leaders must be gentle enough to *comfort the afflicted* and bold enough to *afflict the comforted*. Aim on only one, and our leadership will be ineffective, even destructive. A majority of leaders are good only on one side of the equation.

Some leaders are very gentle to the afflicted; they function like wise counsellors who provide comforting words to those who are heavy-laden but are completely incapable to confront others when the circumstance requires. Permissive leaders will create a permissive work culture where people push the ethical boundaries and prefer asking for forgiveness rather than permission from the top.

Other leaders, however, are squarely the opposite. They exhibit an alpha-like personality, extremely opinionated, intimidating, even abusive towards their followers (more likely male rather than female). They afflict their followers by imposing incredibly high standards and readily confront them if they fall short of them.[2]

It is a tall order to expect leaders to be both gentle and bold. But it should be part of every Christian leader's personal development trajectory. How does God equip them to be able to speak the truth in love? Both the biblical and non-biblical evidences point to one thing. Hardship makes leaders.

The school of suffering provides the best education for leaders; its curriculum is much more formative than any ivy-league business schools. Writing about how God is preparing his green saints in this world before communing in the next with seasoned saints, A.W. Tozer (2015, p. 165) wrote,

> We tend to think of Christianity as a painless system by which we can escape the penalty of past sins and attain to heaven at last. The flaming desire to be rid of every unholy thing and

to put on the likeness of Christ at any cost is not often found among us. We expect to enter the everlasting kingdom of our Father and to sit down around the table with sages, saints and martyrs; and through the grace of God, maybe we shall; yes, maybe we shall.

But for the most of us it could prove at first an embarrassing experience. Ours might be the silence of the untried soldier in the presence of the battle-hardened heroes who have fought the fight and won the victory and who have scars to prove that they were present when the battle was joined.

The devil, things and people being what they are, it is necessary for God to use the hammer, the file and the furnace in His holy work of preparing a saint for true sainthood. It is doubtful whether God can bless a man greatly until He has hurt him deeply.

It is important to acknowledge that hardship in and of itself is evil. Any philosophy that says otherwise is a form of denial. Yet God can turn it into good for our sake and others' sake. When God individually customized our purpose-built suffering, our pain will be met by his healing, our weakness by his strength. As such, the experience of being broken by God is a prerequisite of effective leadership. Talents, skills, opportunities might catapult individuals into prominent leadership roles, but without God's custom-designed crucibles in their lives, their leadership journey will be obstructed by pride, fear, and guilt.

What enabled King David to pen beautiful psalms that nourish countless souls for generations? He could write deeply comforting words like 'The Lord is my shepherd. I shall not want' after going through the experience of being hunted like a fugitive by his psychotic predecessor for fifteen long years.

What qualified the apostle Paul to write more epistles, plant more churches, and penetrate more cities with the gospel? More than the many credentials he had is his partaking in Christ's suffering. Being stoned, beaten, and lashed, to name a few, gave him gentle courage and courageous gentleness to lead and serve the saints.

Christ himself, the God-man, was rendered fitting to be our ever-present help in trouble after he experienced trouble first-hand. 'For because he himself has suffered when tempted, he is able to help those who are being tempted (Hebrew 2:18).

Here is the divine curriculum of Christian leadership development. Christ is formed in you as you bear his comfort-inducing affliction, and Christ is shared through you as you speak the truth in love. The pain we felt and tears we shed, over the unfair criticisms of mean-spirited people are often a means of grace to remove self-pity from our hearts. Only when we love others, we are enabled to speak the truth in love to them. We boldly confront them out of love with words that are true, loving, personal, and appropriate. That is how a leader can be an awfully powerful weapon in the Redeemer's hands.

Notes

1 This quote is attributed to Pastor Alister Begg, who might have mentioned it in one of his sermons.
2 Some of the most well-known and successful business leaders such as Steve Jobs, Jeff Bezos, and Elon Musk are this category. Their organizations may flourish under their leadership but often at the expense of the employees' wellbeing and growth.

References

Baxter, R. (1691). *Directions against inordinate man-pleasing.* https://puritansermons.2a03.party/baxter/baxter6.htm. Accessed May 6, 2019.

Bennis, W. (1994). *On becoming a leader.* Reading, MA: Addison-Wesley.

Crabtree, S. (2011). *Practicing affirmation: God-centered praise of those who are not God.* Crossway.

Eubanks, D. L., Antes, A. L., Friedrich, T. L., Caughron, J. J., Blackwell, L. V., Bedell-Avers, K. E., & Mumford, M. D. (2010). Criticism and outstanding leadership: An evaluation of leader reactions and critical outcomes. *The Leadership Quarterly, 21*(3), 365–388.

Gardner, J. (1990). *On leadership* (p. 135). New York, NY: Free Press.

Keller, T. (2012). *The freedom of self-forgetfulness: The path to true Christian joy.* Chorley, England: 10 Publishing.

Kelley, R. (1988, November). In praise of followership. *Harvard Business Review.*

Morris, L. (2008). *1 Corinthians* (Tyndale New Testament commentaries). IVP Academic.

Owens, B. P., & Hekman, D. R. (2012). Modeling how to grow: An inductive examination of humble leader behaviors, contingencies, and outcomes. *Academy of Management Journal,* 55(4), 787–818.

Tozer, A. W. (2009). *And he dwelt among us: Teaching from the Gospel of John.* Ventura, CA: Regal.

Tozer, A. W. (2015). *The root of the righteous* (Reprint ed.). Moody Publishers.

Welch, E. (1997). *When people are big and God is small: Overcoming peer pressure, codependency, and the fear of man.* P&R Publishing.

CHAPTER 6

Leading with creative tension

*'If you read history you will find that the Christians who did the most
for the present world were precisely those
who thought most of the next.'*

(*C.S. Lewis*)

The name Lee Iacocca is synonymous with golden age of the American automobile industry in the 1980s. His name is immortalized in the hall of fame of American corporate history as the person who turned the Chrysler Corporation around from its near bankruptcy.

A less known fact about Iacocca was his leadership stint at Ford Motor Company between 1946 and 1978 prior to Chrysler. Iacocca hatched a plan to manufacture a car that would weigh no more than 2000 pounds and cost no more than US$2000 called the Ford Pinto (Giampetro-Meyer et al., 1998). Lauded as a noble and grand ambition that would contribute significantly to the great American dream, it was quickly embraced by the stakeholders of the company. Thanks to Iacocca's personal charisma, his personal ambition became a company-wide vision.

Major flaws of safety requirements in the prototype were identified in the design process. The faulty design caused its gasoline tank to be prone to explosion after rear-end collisions. Under the spell of Iacocca's inspiring $2000/2000 pounds ambition, the company, however, proceeded with manufacturing the car despite their awareness of its serious defect.

The decision to proceed was purely economic. Risk assessment and cost-benefit analysis revealed that the cost of implementing a new design to deal with the gas tank design problem was nearly three times higher than the potential liabilities paid out to accident victims. No change was made to the gas tank.

In its first year, the company sold over four hundred thousand Pintos. Then everything went south. Naked ambition for profit comes with a hefty price tag. Numerous accidents and death were reported when the car burst into flames following a rear-end collision, claiming 500 deaths and hundreds of injuries. As many as 117 lawsuits were filed against Ford and almost 1.5 million Ford Pintos were recalled in June 1978. A month later, Iacocca was fired. In a 1979 landmark case in Indiana, Ford Motor Co. became the first American corporation charged with criminal homicide charges.

In his autobiography, Iacocca (1984, p. 172) wrote, 'Whose fault was it? One obvious answer is that it was the fault of Ford's management – including me . . . It seems to me, though, that it is fair to hold management to a high standard and to insist that they do what duty and common sense require, no matter what the pressures.'

The dark side of ambition

As can be seen in Iacocca's case above, it is ambition that prompts leaders to commit unethical, illegal, even destructive behaviors. The very thing that makes individuals rise to greatness has every potential to spiral them downward.

It is ambition that triggers all sorts of manipulative, resume-building behaviors at work. Think about executives or those who pursue leadership roles in high-profile initiatives or high-status boards but delegate all the responsibilities to their staff. Or leaders who hold press conferences to claim the credits for successful projects. In Australia, people who are extremely ambitious are called 'tall poppies'. They are typically resented not so much because they stand taller than others, but because of what they do to show they stand taller than others. As such, they are cut down to the same size as all the others.

There is a clear difference between leaders who are driven by need for achievement and naked ambition. Classic motivation scholars argue achievement-oriented leaders will be happily contented with a job well done while ambitious leaders have their eyes fixated on the prize, i.e., recognition and extrinsic, tangible rewards such as job promotion, pay raises, awards, or public adulation (McClelland, 1961). Achievement-oriented leaders are keen to succeed with some standard of excellence, e.g., conscientiousness, dutifulness, orderliness (McClelland, Atkinson, Clark, & Lowell, 1953, p. 110). In contrast, even though ambitious leaders may have an equally strong desire for achievement, the attainment of the goals may not necessarily be based on superior performance. In other words, ambitious leaders may employ ethically ambiguous means to achieve a legitimate end.

In short, ambition may propel leaders to behave in a Machiavellian manner, engaging in prosocial behaviors if they perceive that doing so will accelerate their goals and interests. They would not hesitate to support initiatives that may be seen as questionable by others (e.g., allowing fast-food companies or 'fizzy' drink manufacturers to sponsor sporting events, despite the negative effects these products have on child obesity and health). In other words, leaders who are ambitious are prone to exemplify 'the end justifies the means' mode of operation.

In an empirical study using case studies, simulations, and survey questionnaires that I conducted with my colleagues on the link between Machiavellian values and leaders' behaviors, we found that they offset the effects of authentic leadership (Sendjaya, Pekerti, Härtel, Hirst, & Butarbutar, 2016). To illustrate this effect, we included a story in our published article in the *Journal of Business Ethics* about Mother Teresa.

Mother Teresa won a Nobel Peace Prize for her authentic moral courage and tenacity to live and work among the poorest of the poor. Not many people were aware however that she received cash donations of more than $1.25 million and frequent access to a private jet in the 1980s from a convicted embezzler, Charles Keating (Padilla, Hogan, & Kaiser, 2007). Keating was convicted of his role in the Savings and Loan multi-million dollar scandal. Notwithstanding this revelation, however, Mother Teresa refused to return the money and wrote a letter on behalf of Keating to the judge pleading for leniency.

While it might be fair to assume that the money has been spent on charity, it did not negate the fact that Mother Teresa used morally ambiguous means to justify the noble cause of helping the less fortunate (i.e., behaving in a Machiavellian manner). As such, she exemplified authentic yet Machiavellian behavior. As this might be a potentially contentious case, we were careful to explain that we did not imply that she invoked the same value-orientation to describe both authentic leadership (other-serving) and Machiavellian (self-serving) behavior. What seems more likely was that she deeply believed the source of money was, at this time, subservient to her cause. Thus, she acted in accordance to her core belief (which made her authentic) despite employing a morally ambiguous means to achieve that end (which made her Machiavellian).

It should be noted that, while receiving funds from tainted sources might constitute an anomalous action for Mother Teresa, one would be hard-pressed to say the same for those in the corporate settings who claim or are perceived to be authentic leaders.

Is ambition always bad?

Nothing great was ever achieved without ambition. The greatest achievements in the history of human progress are products of ambition. It is ambition that causes individuals to attempt the humanly impossible and transcend boundaries known to mankind. It is the ambitious individuals who build great and enduring organizations or fight for noble causes. Think, for example, Steve Jobs and Mohandas Gandhi, respectively (or Lee Iacocca and Mother Teresa, as aforementioned).

However, depending on one's school of thought or personal encounter with it, ambition can be seen either as a virtuous or vicious property. In the management literature, ambition is seen as something positive. Scholars suggest that ambition is a trait that signifies 'the persistent and generalized striving for success, attainment, and accomplishment' (Judge & Kammeyer-Mueller, 2012, p. 759).

Ambitious people show willingness to accept responsibilities, develop plans and goals both professionally and personally, and intentionally make extra efforts to attain them. As such, they have been characterized as individuals who are assertive, confident, and achievement-oriented. They have a strong outlook towards upward mobility.

No doubt we love to follow ambitious leaders. They challenge our capacities, stretch our limits, and extend our imaginations. We need to live for something bigger than ourselves.

On the contrary we tend to ignore non-ambitious leaders. Given enough time we grow frustrated and restless working around them. Their low enthusiasm zaps our energy. We would rather follow blindly ambitious leaders than non-ambitious leaders.

Our non-binding attitude towards ambition is aptly summarized as follows (Champy & Nohria, 2000, p. 1):

> People have always been ambivalent about ambition. We see it as dangerous yet essential. We disapprove of those who abuse it, but we dismiss those who lack it. We see too little of it as a failing, too much of it as a sin. We sense that ambition is combustible, a form of energy that can bring us immortal glory but also destroy us forever, depending on how we use it.

Why moderate ambition is not an option

The aforementioned discussion seems to suggest that there is a curvilinear relationship between leadership ambition and leadership effectiveness. That is, the key to leaders' effectiveness is a moderate level of ambition, sufficient but not excessive. In other words, be ambitious, but not too ambitious. As with everything else, have it in moderation, too little or too much ambition is bad.

That is precisely the sort of advice that is not at all helpful. It is great in theory but nearly impossible in practice. How much ambition is enough? If every new leader has to be injected with the ambition serum, how do we ensure the dosage is right so as to avoid its lethal side effects?

Suppose we are able to know with scientific precision the level of ambition necessary for leadership effectiveness or longevity, how do we ensure that leaders will maintain that level and not go overboard? Leaders who are deeply committed into a specific goal would make endless investments of time and efforts on a daily basis. These investments often become a sunk cost, which by definition cannot be recovered. Typically an escalation of commitment would occur where leaders become over committed to a course of action to the point that they rationalize every blunder. Alternatively, moderate ambition might lead to mediocre performance.

Is there an alternative for Christian leaders? In order to answer this question, we will examine different types of leadership ambition.

Four types of leadership ambitions

The matrix in Figure 6.1 offers a typology of leadership ambition. Technically speaking, they can be a 'continuum' rather than a 'typology' because it is possible to be somewhere in between those four quadrants. However, anecdotal evidences that I have come across thus far suggest that leaders generally display one of the four types quite visibly.

We will briefly look at each quadrant and trace the movement that Christian leaders can experience from the first to the last quadrant.

In the first quadrant, we find Christian leaders who has very low ambition to lead and merely assume they understand the gospel. For these leaders, being in a leadership position is not only a joyless responsibility, but also completely detached from the gospel. They occupy leadership roles because they cannot say no to social

	Natural	Gospel
High	2. Blind, higher ambition leader	4. Gospel-saturated, higher-ambition leader
Low	1. Lower-ambition leader	3. Gospel-sanctified, lower-ambition leader

Figure 6.1 The gospel & ambition matrix

pressures and expectations. According to the regulatory focus theory, this type of leader manifests a prevention focus, which means that what drives them is a sense of duty and avoidance of social rejection, both real and imagined (Brockner & Higgins, 2001).

Leaders who find themselves in this quadrant get through their leadership tenure by doing just the bare minimum. They interact with their staff only as part of formality or when there is a crisis. Under this *laissez faire* leadership, the organization is run on the autopilot mode. Even if we now have self-driving cars on the road that can be programmed not to run downhill, the absence of an alert driver who is willing and able to make instant judgment calls might eventually result in major collisions.

The second quadrant refers to 'the blind, higher-ambition leaders', those who possess raw ambitions and minimal understanding of the gospel. Intensely driven by their ambition for power, status, money, they use their leadership roles simply as a means to be able to satisfy the idols of their hearts. They enjoy being in charge, and naturally prefer being a leader rather than a follower in any given setting. In terms of their self-regulation mechanism, they manifest a promotion focus (as opposed to prevention focus), having their eyes fixed on accomplishments and attainment of rewards.

Their idolatrous ambitions look different in each profession. For entrepreneurs, it is successful start-ups. For professionals, it is the highest position in the corporate hierarchy. For researchers, it is Google scholar citations and competitive grants. For pastors, it is growth in attendance and church services.

'Gospel-sanctified, lower-ambition leaders' in the third quadrant are those whose ambitions have been sanctified with the gospel yet remain visibly low. They realize the God who calls them into a leadership role is the God who will break their sinful ambitions. They are aware that until their natural ambition has been sanctified with Christ, they will never be useful instruments in the hands of the Redeemer.

Yet they have low leadership ambition given their myopic view of the gospel. Sanctified ambition to them means that they no longer have personal ambitions. After all, they now live and work for Christ. In other words, the orientation of their ambitions is changed, their breadth and depth do not. We might know Christian leaders who genuinely love the Lord but whose hearts are not gripped by the global implications of the gospel of the kingdom of God over all creation. We will revisit this phenomenon in subsequent sections.

The fourth quadrant is the ideal typology of Christian leaders whose lives have been deeply and thoroughly touched by the gospel of grace. The gospel compels them not only to have sanctified ambition, but also have it in a large dose rather than small or medium. They can no longer afford to be half-hearted about how they execute the office of leadership entrusted to them. They are compelled to work harder than everyone else on the one hand, yet never allow that intensity and tenacity to erode their humble reliance on the grace of God on a daily basis (see the ambition of the apostle Paul in the box below).

A portrait of gospel-saturated, higher-ambition leader

Thankfully we have a role model in the New Testament from which we can learn how to rightly treat ambition. If there is a list of most ambitious people in the Bible, no doubt the apostle Paul would appear on top. He was ambitious before and after his conversion. He was a zealous persecutor of Christians, going from house to house to drag men and women off to prison. He was miraculously turned into a zealous messenger of the gospel. He wrote at the end of his letter to the Christians in Rome:

> 'from Jerusalem and all the way around to Illyricum I have fulfilled the ministry of the gospel of Christ; and thus I make it my *ambition* to preach the gospel, not where Christ has already been named, lest I build on someone else's foundation.'

> (Romans 15:19–20)

That succinct and modest sentence encapsulates a long decade of strenuous labor for Christ, which included three missionary journeys covering 1400 miles from what would be today Tel Aviv in Jerusalem to Tirana in Albania. He planted the seeds of the gospel in most populous cities of his time, enduring much physical and emotional suffering in the more civilized parts of the Roman Empire. He made it his ambition to boldly go where no man has gone before to preach the Gospel. He logged more miles, planted more churches, and trained more church leaders than any other person in his generation. He co-authored at least half of the entire books in the New Testament.

It was ambition that saw Paul enduring multiple rounds of thirty-nine lashes from the enemies of the cross. After ten years of repeated beatings to his body and ego, rather than thinking of sabbatical leave or early retirement, he turned his eyes on the next ambitious frontier, saying to the Roman Christians, 'Help me to win Spain with the Gospel of Christ!' Paul considered his countless near-death experiences a brief walk in a polluted park in comparison to the eternal and weighty glory he would enjoy in the new city of God.

When God decided to appoint someone to represent him to the uncharted territory of the Greco-Roman world, he did not choose the most loving apostle like John or the most eloquent apostle like Peter. He chose the most ambitious person like Paul. What made him super-resilient was not his intellect, talents, or humility. It was his ambition. His Spirit-sanctified, Christ-centered, God-magnifying ambition. God bestowed a sufficient dose of grace for this ambitious earthen vessel so that God's awesome power can be seen most visibly as he breaks that jar of clay.

But as his team, Timothy, Titus, Silas, and many others saw first-hand, he never rooted his identity in his ambition or the success of achieving it. His identity is securely attached to the undeserved mercy of God that he had received as, by his own admission, the chief of sinners. He owed God his life, as such his life was driven by one singular ambition to give more and more to Christ, who has given him everything he could ever give.

If there is one thing we can learn about ambition from the apostle Paul, it is that nothing great in God's kingdom is ever achieved without a gospel-sanctified and gospel-saturated ambition. God will not and cannot use a self-ambitious person. Yet he also never uses a zero-ambition person. Like the staff is Moses' hand, he will take our ambitions, set them aside, and repurpose them for a greater cause. There is no telling how history will turn and twist when that occurs.

This type of leadership ambition goes beyond the 'management visioning', i.e., guided reflection to imagine a clear, mental picture of an ideal reality. Many well-meaning consultants typically advise that we need to know the core purpose of a company beyond the unique differentiators and value propositions it offers. But a gospel-saturated ambition is not merely about drawing a great vision.

It is also not about embracing the popular productivity mantra of our day. If you are an avid reader of self-help books, you will be familiar with the following catchphrase. 'Begin with an end in mind', 'Start with why', 'Big hairy audacious goals', 'Purpose-driven life', to name a few. These might be helpful concepts, and have been used by wise career advisers to help us identify the difference between building a resume and leaving a legacy, and the importance to do the former without losing sight of the latter.

While these are positive and well-meaning advices that many can benefit from, if they are not linked to the gospel of Jesus Christ, they never go beyond the boundaries of time and space of the present, fallen world. As the book of Ecclesiastes reminds us, life under the sun is marred with meaningless and frustration. In the final analysis, decoupled from the gospel, our lofty ambition under the sun are akin to building a better mousetrap in a run-down building. The gospel however points us to gaze beyond the sun, and marvel at the One who comes from beyond it, has come and died under it, but was raised beyond it.

In the subsequent sections we will deal with the more practical issue of how to move from the first to the last quadrant. That is, how Christian leaders have gospel-saturated ambitions.

A disclaimer might be warranted here. The next section might read like a major detour from the subject of leadership ambition. It is not. We will look at the grand story of redemption in which we find our personal and collective stories. It is the story God is weaving our lives into from the early pages of the book of Genesis. It is a sensemaking frame to understand the place of ambition in the meta-narrative of human history.

The origin story

When Satan inhabited the serpent, the most cunning and shrewd animal in all of God's creation, to carry out his plans to deceive Adam and Eve, he planted the seed of raw, anti-God ambitions in humans. He first twisted what God said by falsely claiming that God did forbid Adam and Eve to eat not just one fruit, but any fruit in the garden. Satan's strategic objective was to portray God as a cosmic killjoy and raise skepticism of God's goodness towards his creation.

Instead of confronting the lies of the serpent there and then, the woman was drawn into the deceitful mind game by adding that they were not supposed to even touch the fruit (something which God never said). When the serpent saw that he got the woman's attention in the deception game, he further enticed her by planting two desires in her mind: 'You will not certainly die' and 'You will be like God'.

The two desires forever tempt every Christian ever since. They were the seeds of what we now consider natural human ambitions. We have seen various attempts in the history of human progress to not die and be like God. Many breakthroughs in biology and medicine, for example, have been largely shaped by the ambition to preserve life and to be self-sufficient without God.

God has every right to say what is good and what is not good because he is the Creator God. In the creation account, God saw that all the things he created were good. He also declared that it was not good for man to be alone, and it was certainly not good for the man and woman to eat the fruit of the tree of the knowledge of good and evil. The point is we need to rely on God to tell us what is good and what is evil, and the just consequence of ignoring it.

When the woman, followed by her husband, was filled with the ambition to be like God, she declared her independence from God. She essentially said, 'Things are different now. I don't need you to tell me what is good and what is evil. I get to decide what I can or can't do, and am pretty sure now won't die for trying'.

Thankfully that was not the entire story. In the midst of that dark and treacherous trajectory, God's grace appeared. Immediately after the fall, God initiated a search and rescue mission. In a gracious and straightforward manner, he asked Adam, 'Where are you?' The question did not imply that God did not have the latitude and longitude of Adam's whereabouts. When God asks a question to someone in the Bible, he does that not because he does not have the answer, but because the person needs to be asked.

Instead of repenting from their outright disobedience and pleading for forgiveness, Adam and Eve descended into what has since become a very familiar pattern today: Blaming others to justify self. What followed was tragic but not unexpected. The just consequences of sin were spelled out, namely pain and misery in three life domains: work, childbearing, marital relationships.

Let's take the domain of work, and consider two examples. First, we ignored the cultural mandate to cultivate the resources that God generously gave as part of the created order. Instead filled with the blind ambition to conquer the world, we exploit them for short-term and personal gain. We should not be shocked to find ourselves dealing with issues like climate change, global poverty, and income inequality. These are the deaths we slowly experience for throwing God's principle of stewardship out of the window.

We also blissfully ignore the pattern and importance of Sabbath rest, and choose to become a workaholic society. We think that working harder, smarter, and longer will make us better and stronger. The consequences are dire. People experience all kinds of death in the workplace in the name of growth and productivity. Repeated studies show that there is an increasing rate of burnout, depression, alienation, discrimination, and bullying in today's workplaces.

The judgment God gave to Satan for tempting his image bearers was swift. But it was in the middle of that judgment, we learnt that he is truly a merciful and long-suffering God. He pronounced the enmity between the seed of the woman and the seed of the serpent, but there was something divine with it. At the fall, the man and woman renounced friendship with God and made an alliance with Satan. But God turned that friendship with Satan into enmity. What it really meant was God restored the friendship with his image bearers. He sided with them despite their rebellion.

The rest, as they say, is history. The enmity between the seed of the woman and the seed of the serpent has been unfolded across generations. Starting with the first murder involving Cain and Abel, the enmity was seen in the sagas between the Israelites and the Egyptians, David and Goliath, until it reached the climax in the face off between Jesus Christ and Satan in multiple accounts in the four gospels. The anticlimactic pattern continued with the persecution of the Roman government towards the early church, and the hostilities that the church of Jesus Christ has endured until today.

The enmity is real, but God has promised victory to his people. In what is known as 'proto-evangelium' or 'first gospel', God declared that the seed of the woman (i.e., Jesus Christ, cf. Galatians 4:4) will crush the serpent's head, whilst his heel will be crushed by Satan on the cross. Jesus crushed the serpent's head by bearing the judgement of God upon Adam, and thereby taking Adam's sin, shame, and guilt on himself.

In the same chapter, we also read that God clothed Adam and Eve with garments of skin to replace the fig leaves. Blood of an animal was shed to make the garments of skin possible. That was the first of many bloody animal sacrifices in the long history of elaborate rituals that God instituted for his people for one objective. They point to Jesus, the 'Lamb of God who takes away the sin of the world' (John 1:29), the blameless and ultimate bloody sacrifice for our sins, for 'without shedding of blood there is no forgiveness of sins' (Hebrew 9:22).

That is why today Christians everywhere are invited to the Lord's table on the Lord's day to 'take and eat' the body of Christ. That is, to be strengthened spiritually by Christ's special presence among his people symbolized by the bread served at the table. Note that the phrase 'take and eat' was initially the language of rebellion, for the woman 'took and ate' the fruit of the forbidden tree. The verbs of rebellion became the verbs of salvation when Christ took and drank the cup of God's wrath on the cursed tree.

How the gospel sanctifies ambitions

The above origin story of the first gospel has a clear implication on individual believers. By taking Adam's sin upon himself, Christ saves us from ourselves, sin, and death. We no longer live for ourselves but for Christ who for our sake died and was raised (cf. 2 Corinthians 5:14–15). This individual dimension of the gospel is built around the idea of personal salvation.

In a typical mainstream church, the bulk of Christian education is concentrated around the following sequential teaching pattern – God, sin, Christ, faith. What these four big words unpack is the rich systematic theology of God's search and rescue mission. God created his image bearers with the capacity to obey him; we rebelled against God, replacing him with a pseudo-god in oblivion of the hell-bound consequences; Christ came to seek and save us from ourselves, sin, and death; we respond to him in faith to be saved for eternity with God.

The individual lens from which the gospel is often understood as above is absolutely necessary, but biblically insufficient. There are a few reasons why they are insufficient. For example, it assumes the presence of marred conscience and haunting guilt as a consequence of the truth claim that disobedience to God leads to sin. That assumption may be readily accepted as given by previous generations. Today the biblical categories of truth, sin, and guilt simply do not exist in the minds of postmodern people. They have polar opposite understanding of them, i.e., truth is relative, sin is a social construction of morality, and guilt is an emotional weakness.

But the most salient reason why the individual perspective is insufficient is that it puts man as the central purpose of God's grace and mercy. While this may not necessarily lead to hubris, it neglects the bigger, cosmic story of God renewing the entire creation. We might readily accept that as new creation in Christ, our whole person renewal – mind, emotion, will – includes our ambition, and that our ambition is radically transformed from its natural (and often sinful) stage. But to what end? If Christ transforms the Christian leaders' ambition through his death and resurrection, what is the end goal?

The redemptive-historical perspective of the gospel

In order to have a proper understanding of Christian leadership ambition, we need to re-shape its trajectory. To that end, we need to look beyond the individual dimension of the gospel. We need to grasp its corporate dimension or, stated in more fancy term, its redemptive-historical perspective.

The redemptive-historical perspective is often applied in the field of hermeneutics and homiletics. Underpinning the redemptive-historical perspective is the progressive revelation of God's plan of renewing the creation through his mighty acts and prophetic words through the lives of appointed human agents, which finds its eschatological fulfilment in Christ. It is a perspective that looks at the whole counsel of God in light of Jesus Christ.

The redemptive-historical organizing framework includes creation, fall, redemption, new creation. God created us to be co-cultivators and co-creators in his good world; we dethroned God and took his place, causing sin and evil to be deeply embedded within every fabric of the society; Christ came to redeem the world through his death and resurrection; Christ will return to renew all creation, eradicate evil, and restore absolute peace and justice in the world.

Without this meta-narrative, it is easy for us to get off track or side tracked. But once we grasp it, we are better equipped to see the eternal significance of our work as leaders. More practically speaking, if the individual dimension of the gospel tells us, 'Christ loves you so much he saved you from hell so you can enjoy him forever both in this world and the next,' the corporate dimension of the gospel tells us, 'Christ loves you so much he saved you from this fallen world so you can help renew it in the strength of and collaboration with Christ.'

The new creation is implied in the *proto-evangelium* narrative outlined above. Creation fell when Adam sinned. It was subjected to futility (Romans 8:20). It has not fulfilled the purpose for which it was made. The good news is it will be transformed when God's children will be completely transformed.

When Christ crushes the serpent's head, the victory over sin that Christ secures extends, as the Christmas hymn reminds us every year, 'far as the curse is found'. The Earth should rejoice not only at the first coming of her King, but also (more so) at his second coming when he reigns supreme over his renewed creation. If there is a square inch in the most remote boundaries of the curse that is out of reach, Christ's redemptive work would be incomplete. In the words of Plantinga (2002, p. 96):

> If all has been created good and all has been corrupted, then all must be redeemed. God isn't content to save souls; God wants to save bodies too. God isn't content to save human beings in their individual activities; God wants to save social systems and economic structures too.

Both the systematic-theological perspective (i.e., God-Man-Christ-Faith) and the redemptive-historical perspective (Creation-

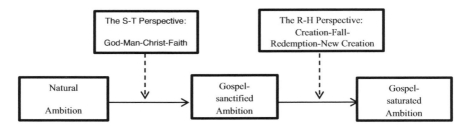

Figure 6.2 The progression of gospel-shaped ambition

Fall-Redemption-New Creation) of the gospel are critical, yet the latter is completely foreign to many. We think that the former is more personally relatable and practically useful. This is the reason why an overwhelming majority of Christian leaders have a lop-sided understanding of the gospel, and run into the grave danger of neutralizing its effects.

To move beyond this anemic view of the gospel and thought-fully understand its full ramifications on our public life, we need to have a deep knowledge of the redemptive-historical perspective. If we are acutely aware of God's cosmic mission in renewing the world, and that it is still an unfinished mission to date, it ought to shape our sanctified ambitions this side of heaven.

As a quick recap of our discussion thus far, Figure 6.2. depicts the relationship between leadership ambition and the gospel. Note the sequential pattern of how our ambition is transformed by the gospel. The systematic-theological perspective of the gospel helps us to have our ambitions sanctified in, with, and for Christ. The redemptive-historical perspective of the gospel helps us to saturate that sanctified ambitions with the gospel.

Gospel-saturated ambition

In this section, drawing on the central notion of Herman Bavinck's theology (i.e., 'grace restores nature'), we will examine how the gospel actually saturates our ambitions. 'Grace restores nature' is a shorthand that points to the gospel as the good news that the grace of God in Christ Jesus restores the corrupted world as far as the curse is found. Bavinck (1989, p. 61) succinctly puts it as follows:

Christianity does not introduce a single substantial foreign element into the creation. It creates no new cosmos but rather makes the cosmos new. It restores what was corrupted by sin.

The gospel is not a story of God's second attempt at creation. It is a story of God's restoration of the first one. He does not create a new world, but makes the world new. God did not devise a 'Plan B' after the fall. He maintained his original purpose in the created order, which is why he sent his Son to restore the fallen world to its initial design.

In modern day business parlance, we call an executive who could take a failing organization and repair it to a functioning even profitable stage a 'turnaround artist'. God is the ultimate turnaround artist – he is reclaiming the broken world in Christ Jesus, restoring it to its original condition, in fact making it better.

When Jesus healed the sick and raised the dead during his ministry on earth, he did not only demonstrate his mercy towards them or his sovereignty over sickness and death. He was also restoring of the broken world to its original design where sickness and death have no part of. When he turned water into wine in Cana, he did not merely show his love and power, he was telling us that there will be no more disappointment, mourning, crying, and pain in the city of God, only pure and everlasting joy.

That ideal intent and design is what the biblical authors calls 'shalom'. Shalom in the truest biblical sense refers to something much deeper and broader than mere absence of external conflict or presence of internal peace of mind. Based on the vision seen by Isaiah and other biblical prophets (cf. Isaiah 60:11–21; 65:15–25), Plantinga (1995, p. 10) defines shalom as follows:

> In the Bible, shalom means universal flourishing, wholeness, and delight – rich state of affairs in which natural needs are satisfied and natural gifts fruitfully employed, a state of affairs that inspires joyful wonder as its Creator and Savior opens doors and welcomes the creatures in whom he delights. Shalom, in other words, is the way things ought to be.

Because God's shalom has been vandalized in the present and fallen world, Christian leaders are called to be agents of shalom, restoring proper relationships not only between God and humans, but also humans with each other, and humans with nature.

> The gospel is the news that distorted patterns of power have been broken: the reception of the gospel is the embrace of radically transformed patterns of social relationships.
>
> (Brueggemann, 1993, p. 34)

We should operate in every sphere within the created order. We should in obedient gratitude to God and imitation of Christ work for the renewal of human life towards the design God meant it to be.

> Biblical hope has a wide-angle lens. It takes in the whole nations and peoples. It brings into focus the entire created order – wolves and lambs, mountains and plains, rivers and valleys. When it is widest and longest, biblical hope looks forward towards a whole 'new heaven and new earth' in which the death, and mourning, and pain will have passed away (Rev 21:1,4), and in which the Son of God receives the treasures of nations who parade into the city of God (Rev 21:22–26).
>
> (Plantinga, 2002, p. 14)

The more we occupy our minds with this eschatological vision of the gospel, the more we are encouraged to work wholeheartedly for the Lord in this side of heaven. What we do this side of heaven in the name of Christ truly matter, for they will be part of the 'treasures of nation' in the new Jerusalem.

Practically speaking, what does it mean today for Christian leaders? Our view of work, both as leaders and followers, should be profoundly transformed. The dualistic sacred-secular, clergy-laity, Sunday-Monday view should be jettisoned altogether in light of this eschatological vision. With the reformers, we affirm the belief that every occupation offered as a sacrifice to God is as holy and pure as those found in the monasteries.

Work no longer serves as a necessary evil for survival, a strategy for self-actualization, or merely a platform for evangelism. Rather, work becomes a thoughtful engagement for God's shalom to penetrate to the vandalized world as it is being restored in Christ.

Because the meaning of work is radically transformed, we would prayerfully and wisely choose the type of profession, industry, and organizations we will be working in. The prospect of money, status, or power no longer becomes a decisive factor. Instead, it is a matter of strategic choice where we can contribute the most to the world-renewing agenda of God. In the words of Wolterstorff (1983, p. 17), 'If each of us is to reshape his or her occupation into a channel of obedience, then presumably each of us must also search for that occupation which will best serve as a channel of obedience.'

Becoming a team leader in a small start-up or a global conglomerate group is a thoughtful and spiritual service to God because 'a career turned toward this world with God behind one's back is not inferior to a career toward God' (Wolterstorff, 1983, p. 17).

Our work to restore the image of God in places where that image has been lost becomes important. We speak up for those who cannot speak for themselves, defend the rights of those who are being systematically marginalized, confront perpetrators of evil and injustice, and comfort those who have fallen captive to idolatry. We will also be more sensitive to the temptation to overwork and underwork.

Leading with creative tension

Christian leaders whose ambitions have been saturated with the gospel will lead with creative tension. The 'tension' in this context refers to the gap between the current and future reality, between what is and what should be. We live as God's redeemed people in between the first and second coming of Christ.

While through the cross of Christ we are always reminded of, in John Owen's memorable words, the death of death in the death of Christ, the victory is not complete until he returns. There will come a day when God will put an end to all rule and power at Christ's return (1 Corinthians 15:24). There is no more death, mourning, crying, or pain (Revelation 21:4).

We need to constantly remind ourselves of this eschatological vision of the gospel because we live in between the 'already' and 'not yet'. We live in between the kingdom of God that has come ('already') and the kingdom of God that is still to come ('not yet'), between Good Friday and Easter Sunday, between the cross and the resurrection.

In fact, this gap creates 'creative tension'. Creative tension occurs where two contrasting conditions spur the emergence of new and useful ideas. The creative tension between the dark realities of the present state of the fallen world where sin reigns and the future eschatological vision of the renewed world where shalom reigns should compel Christian leaders to work harder and smarter in their respective fields.

Sent to the fallen world as vulnerable sheep in the midst of wolves, to use the simile used by Christ, Christian leaders cannot afford to be clueless and evil, instead they need to be wise as serpents and blameless as doves.

Dr. Martin Luther King Jr. understood the importance of leading with creative tension when he led the struggle to eradicate racism in America. From a collection of letters that he wrote in prison, which was later captured in the book *Letter from Birmingham Jail* (1963), he wrote:

> Just as Socrates felt it was necessary to create a tension in the minds of men so that individuals could rise from the bondage of myths and half-truths; so must we create the kind of tension in society that will help men rise from the dark depths of prejudice and racism.

Prejudice and racism are part of that vandalism of shalom that Christian leaders should work tirelessly to eradicate because we know they are not supposed to be part of God's initial design. They rear their ugly heads in the city of man, but will exist no more in the city of God. In the words of Catherine Booth, co-founder of the Salvation Army, 'If we are to better the future, we must disturb the present.'

The apostle Paul called this tension 'groaning'. The whole creation has been groaning in the pains of childbirth, and we too groan inwardly as we wait eagerly for our full redemption in Christ (Romans 8:22–23). There is a tension between present suffering and the future glory, although the hope of future glory makes that present suffering bearable. In fact, Paul puts things in perspective when he characterized the challenges he faced in his leadership as 'light and momentary troubles' in light of the far greater, eternal glory they are producing in him. He stated the creative tension in his leadership as follows, 'So we fix our eyes not on what is seen, but on what is unseen, since what is seen is temporary, but what is unseen is eternal' (2 Corinthians 4:17–18).

This creative tension between what is seen and what is unseen is something that Christian leaders have to grasp. If we solely focus on what is seen, this evil-ridden world will make us feel frustrated, helpless, and hopeless. If we gaze too intensely on what is unseen, we will be delusional hermits who try to avoid the world altogether. It has been well said that some people are too earthly-minded they are not fit for heaven, whilst some others are too heavenly-minded they are not of much use on earth.

Leading with creative tension, therefore, implies a paradigmatic shift 'from the vision and practice of turning away from the social world in order to seek closer union with God to the vision and practice of working to reform the social world in obedience to God' (Wolterstorff, 1983, p. 11). Into this fallen world, we are called to join a movement to overthrow the present value systems of the world ('cosmos' in Greek) that are hostile to God. In the oft-quoted words of C.S. Lewis (1952, p. 46):

> That's what this world is – enemy occupied territory. Christianity is the story of how the rightful King has landed, you might say, in disguise, and is calling us to take part in a great campaign of sabotage.

This campaign of sabotage is what sensible Christian leaders would do given the presence of evil in the structures, systems, values, and institutions of our society. Careful exegesis of the biblical concept of 'cosmos' in the New Testament reveals the social structuring of evil in the very fabric of our social existence (Mott, 1982). The social apparatus within which we operate as a society has been around long before we came and will be around long after we are gone.

Christian leaders in business must be acutely aware that from the very first full-time job interview until their retirement celebration, they operate in an intricate social structure built by conscious individual decisions of previous generations that were most likely shaped by profit maximization and pursuit of power. Here is a scenario that might describe the personal experiences of countless Christian business leaders (Mott, 1982, p. 10):

> An individual director may have regret regarding the impact that his or her company's pursuit of profits has on the poor in developing countries but feels that there is no use in resisting the process. If one is not willing to do it, he or she will be replaced by someone who is; and if the company stopped the practice, other companies would continue so that the first company would face disaster in a few years in terms of profits and stockholders. They are caught up in a web of obligations and a competitive structure that knows no mercy.

We often feel disenfranchised by the vicious circle of structural evil in corporate bureaucracy that runs on the philosophy of 'greed is good'. But because of the gospel of Christ Jesus, we cannot afford to do nothing.

> We serve a different order, the Reign of Christ, which he sets up in contrast to the prevailing way of life in the social order as supported by the fallen powers . . . We are to follow the Lordship of Christ who judges the world and conquers it . . . By faith we live in Christ's victory, yet we must continue to struggle.
>
> (Mott, 1982, p. 18)

This struggle, campaign of sabotage, creative tension, or whatever else it is called, is not an option for those who have their allegiance to Christ. It is both an individual and corporate responsibility.

> The saints are responsible for the structure of the social world in which they find themselves. The structure is not simply part of the order of nature; to the contrary, it is the result of human decision, and by concerted effort it can be altered. Indeed, it should be altered, for it is a fallen structure.
>
> (Wolterstorff, 1983, p. 3)

We are responsible for the pervasiveness of evil in this deteriorating world by virtue of our nature as the salt of the earth and the light of the world. Indeed, salt and light are two powerful metaphors of leadership. If the one-word definition of leadership is 'influence', then Christian leaders need to influence the social context within which they operate by preventing the moral decay and overcoming the darkness as light. When the world goes awry, it is because Christians do not function as they should. Contaminated salt is not only useless as preservatives or fertilizers, it is corrosive and poisonous; they must be thrown on the road. Similarly, an oil lamp that is put under a basked will not be of much use. We would be wise to heed these sobering words at length of the late Anglican scholar-pastor, John Stott (1984, p. 67):

> Our Christian habit is to bewail the world's deteriorating standards with an air of rather self-righteous dismay. We criticize its violence, dishonesty, immorality, disregard for human life, and materialistic greed. 'The world is going down the drain,' we say with a shrug. 'But whose fault is it? Who is to blame?' Let me put it like this. If the house is dark when night fall comes, there is no sense in blaming the house, for that is what happens when the sun goes down. The question to ask is 'Where is the light?' If the meat goes bad and becomes inedible, there is no sense blaming the meat, for that is what happens when bacteria are left alone to breed. The question to ask is 'Where is the salt?' Just so, if society deteriorates and its standards decline, till it becomes like a dark night or stinking fish, there is no sense in blaming society, for that is what happens when fallen men and women are left to themselves, and human selfishness is unchecked. The question to ask is 'Where is the church? Why are the salt and light of Jesus Christ not permeating and changing our society?' It is sheer hypocrisy on our part to raise our eyebrows, shrug our shoulders or wring our hands. The Lord Jesus told us to be the world's salt and light. If, therefore, darkness and rottenness abound, it is our fault and we must accept the blame.

Next, we will examine three practical implications for leaders who are leading with creative tension. If we have a gospel-saturated ambition to lead with creative tension, how does it inform our decisions, mold our thoughts, and change our behaviors on a daily basis?

1. Simultaneously optimistic and pessimistic

Our accurate grasp of the gospel will spike the level of both our optimism and pessimism. They will be off the charts.

If we believe that one day God will renew this material world and wipe away every tear from our eyes, we will be the most optimistic person in the world. Because we see the light at the end of the tunnel and lo and behold, that light is the supreme and all-embracing reign of God over the restored world. No more cancer, depression, malnourished children, human trafficking, racism, bullying, inequality, and religious conflicts because 'justice rolls down like waters, and righteousness like an ever-flowing stream' (Amos 5:24).

That vantage point is what makes Christian leaders very optimistic. As we are out in front mobilizing and empowering others to redeem the world's systems, culture, and structure for Christ, our prime advantage is not our strength, talent, or experience. After all, we are not stronger, smarter, or wiser than non-Christian leaders, and therefore are entitled to that special anointing from God. What keeps us going when the going gets tough is that certainty of the end of history when Christ returns and reclaims what is rightfully his. As we cling towards that hope, Christ through his spirit within us enables us to joyfully strive in a long obedience in the same direction. C.S. Lewis (1952, p. 134) aptly puts it this way:

> If you read history you will find that the Christians who did the most for the present world were precisely those who thought most of the next . . . It is since Christians have largely ceased to think of the other world that they have become so ineffective in this.

On the other hand, gospel-saturated ambition will turn us into the most pessimistic leaders. No matter how hard we try to fight poverty and corruption, or achieve any one of the United Nations' seventeen sustainable development goals (SDGs), every tiny or major progress we make will be tainted by the prevalence of sins in both individuals and institutions. Each progress will be slow and frustrating. Each progress might be followed by a regress. The more we understand how deep the rabbit hole goes, the more we are ready to embrace the fact that all the good we have been doing for years might be undone by others in the blink of an eye. Such is the nature of progress in the world filled with thistle and thorns.

The gospel makes peculiar leaders. Leaders who will acknowledge that the cup in their hands are both half empty and half full. They know they are sinners leading other sinners in a sin-full world, yet they turn their eyes upon Jesus, who is making all things new. They know their achievements will be quickly forgotten in two generations, but those achievements matter in Christ who is renewing all creation through them.

They have a gloom-ridden take on the prospect that any significant and lasting change can come from political programs, technological advances, or medical breakthroughs. Yet they would be jumping up and down in high grade optimism of the prospect that things will be a thousand times better than the present situation despite the bleak economic and environmental prognosis of the world. They do not have much faith in humanity but possess a rock-solid faith in the divine-human savior.

2. Simultaneously content and discontent

At its core, leadership is about moving people from point A to point B (whereas management is about handling people at one point). As such, by definition, leaders have a sense of deep discontentment with the status quo. The reason effective leaders never make up the majority is because an overwhelming majority of individuals have been socially conditioned to accept mediocrity. Why bother walking the extra mile if everyone else seems to walk on the spot without moving an inch forward?

The apostle Paul was experiencing discontentment when he wrote that Christ compelled him to pursue perfection rather than complacency. Being perfect here does not mean zero defect, but dogged persistence to strain towards the goal, 'Not that I have already obtained this or am already perfect, but I press on to make it my own, because Christ Jesus has made me his own' (Philippians 3:12).

He would agree with Thomas Carlyle who once quipped, 'I've got a great ambition to die of exhaustion rather than boredom.' Towards his pursuit of Christlikeness through personal experience of suffering for and with Christ, Paul would be more than happy to die of exhaustion.

Curiously in the next few verses, Paul wrote that he was also a deeply contented person,

> '. . . for I have learned in whatever situation I am to be content. I know how to be brought low, and I know how to abound. In any and every circumstance, I have learned the secret of facing plenty and hunger, abundance and need.'

He was saying that being in abundance and being in need have little effect for him because his sufficiency was in Christ.

What a stark contrast to Jordan Belfort (2007), the reckless Wall Street trader and stockbroker who infamously said, 'Let me tell you something. There's no nobility in poverty. I've been a rich man and I've been a poor man. And I choose rich every time' [slightly edited to remove profanity].

One chose to be content, the other the riches of the world. One chose Christ the fountain of living waters, the other the broken cisterns that can hold no water. Whose advice do we tend to follow: Apostle Paul or Jordan Belfort? Interestingly both of them ended up in prison for completely different reasons. For Paul, Christ is enough, so he risked everything to experience more of Christ. For Belfort, money is never enough, so he risked everything to obtain more of it.

But note even for Paul that contentment did not come naturally. He had to learn it the hard way, that is through the experiences of being famished, fatigued, threatened, imprisoned, flogged, and stoned (2 Corinthians 11:23–29), each of which functions like a windshield wiper that removes rain, ice, and debris from our life's front window so we can clearly see and experience that Christ is enough.

For many of us today, the suffering we experience is much lesser in intensity and quantity relative to Paul's. It may involve emotional, psychological, and other non-physical sufferings because of our faith in Christ. That may include the experience of being passed over for promotion, shunned away by a key client, or alienated by colleagues. But until we are brought to the point where Christ is all we have, we will never know that he is enough.

However if we are honest to ourselves, we will find that it is almost our second nature to have a misplaced discontentment and contentment. We are discontented with our entitlements and rights, always striving to get the next level of comfort or status. Yet when it comes to experiencing Christ, we rest on our laurels, unwilling to scale new heights for the sake of Christ.

Where we have contentment and discontentment is a reliable indicator of our longevity as leaders. Leaders are built to flip, not built to last, precisely because of their misguided contentment and discontentment. We should be content because what we *have* in Christ today is always enough. On the other hand, we should be discontent because what we *know* about Christ today is never enough.

Granted no Christian leaders possess superhuman strength. Moses, Elijah, and Job were among the saints of old who asked the Lord to end their lives. There are times in our leadership journeys when we might feel the same. But like the apostle Paul, let us learn not to allow external circumstances, good (e.g., six-salary figure, first-rate facilities) or bad (e.g., bullying superiors, difficult people, toxic work culture) to control our leadership attitude and enthusiasm, for we can do all things through Christ who strengthens us.

3. Simultaneously hardworking and relaxed

We have seen above from Paul's letter to the believers in Rome that he was a most ambitious leader, working tirelessly as a trailblazer in the gospel mission. To the believers in Colossae, he wrote something similar:

> Him we proclaim, warning everyone and teaching everyone with all wisdom, that we may present everyone mature in Christ. For this I toil, struggling with all his energy that he powerfully works within me.
>
> (Colossians 1:28–29)

The word for 'toil' refers to labor to the point of weariness. He wore himself out to ensure that Christlikeness would be the number one goal for the believers, even though it meant he would not be the most popular person in the crowd. But he did not stop there. To the believers in Corinth, he even had the audacity to say that he worked harder than his peers.

> But by the grace of God I am what I am, and his grace toward me was not in vain. On the contrary, I worked harder than any of them, though it was not I, but the grace of God that is with me.
>
> (1 Corinthians 15:10)

What a display of gospel-saturated ambition! Relatively speaking, he exerts more efforts than every single person in the apostolic band, doing above and beyond even though he knew full well that the Corinthians would question and attack his motive for being so conscientious. Further, unlike other false teachers of his day, Paul engaged in manual labor as a tent-maker so he did not have to burden the new church he was planting with the responsibility to support him financially.

Yet that was not an ugly show of hubris, for he was humble enough to acknowledge that his industriousness did not originate with him. It was a function of God's grace working fully in him. The grace that turned him from a persecutor of God's people into their most energetic shepherd.

On the other hand, Paul was no workaholic. He can be simultaneously the most hardworking and relaxed individual. In his letter to believers in Thessalonica, Paul exhorted them to 'make it your ambition to lead a quiet life' (1 Thessalonians 4:11). This is the third occurrence of the word 'ambition' in the Greek New Testament (the two other times, as delineated above, are 2 Corinthians 5:9 and Romans 15:20). In his commentary of this verse, Morris (1984, p. 87) paraphrased it as follows, 'Make it your ambition to be unambitious' or 'Seek restlessly to be still'.

To put it differently, there is a place for being completely calm and relaxed in Christian leadership. We do not have to feel guilty when we relax. We do not have to eat the bread of anxious toil. The psalmist aptly puts it this way, 'Nisi Dominus frustra, without the

Lord, frustration' (Psalm 127:1). Of course, countless leaders with complete disregard of God seem to reach a progressively higher level of success every year. They rise up early because it is the early bird that gets the worm, and they go late to rest burning the midnight oil because if they snooze, they lose. Or so they think. But as the psalmist affirms, their hard work is likely to be in vain for three possible reasons.

First, without the Lord, their success might be short-lived given various man-made or natural disasters (e.g., stock market crash, tsunami). Without the Lord, their success is subject to the law of diminishing return – the satisfaction they derive deteriorates as fast as their hunger for more prestigious titles, investment property, or academic journal publications. Without the Lord, their success might turn them into completely different individuals – self-ambitious, self-righteous, cunning, narcissistic, etc.

Not surprisingly, however, with increasing work demands and pressures, many leaders increasingly adopt the attitude 'I'll sleep when I'm dead' (which is the title of a research article by Barnes, 2011).

If there is one thing that can readily accelerate leadership effectiveness, it is for leaders to have more shut eye. Sleep deprivation is a serious leadership issue, and has been found to impair the functioning of structures in the brain that are critical to self-regulation (Barber, Barnes, & Carlson, 2013). Depleted self-regulation in turn will negatively affect cognitive performance (Lim & Dinges, 2010), which then led to unethical behaviors (Barnes, Schaubroeck, Huth, & Ghumman, 2011). A more recent study in fact found that leaders' abusive behaviors fluctuate daily on the basis of their sleep quality (the difficulty of falling and staying asleep) (Barnes, Lucianetti, Bhave, & Christian, 2015).

Many helpful, practical advice has been offered to mitigate the issue of sleep deficiency, from avoiding the use of smartphone at night, psychological treatment such as stimulus-control therapy, and reduced job demands. Christian leaders have the gospel as a deeper resource to help them to be most relaxed individuals, and hence are emotionally and cognitively capable to have better sleep quantity and quality.

Our Creator God has intentionally fashioned us with a body that needs to sleep daily, not weekly, monthly, or biannually. The reason is deceptively simple. We need daily reminders that we are frail and limited creatures. That we are not God. To neglect the gift of sleep is self-worship, resulting in the suffering of our mood and deterioration of our health. Sleeping is an act of worship; we humbly surrender to the One who will neither slumber nor sleep (Psalm 121:4). When our daily work is done, to paraphrase Victor Hugo, we can go to sleep in peace because God is awake.

Sleeping is also an act of faith, for the Lord gives to his beloved in their sleep. True productivity is ultimately not about working hard, or working smarter. To be productive is to do our God-appointed lot daily, stop, and then go to bed in faith. Sleeping is declaring that what matters is not the builders who labor, but the Lord who builds for he can do far more in my sleep than my best efforts in my most-productive, highly caffeinated day.

Sleeping is an act of resistance to the world who gives us endless stimuli to be anxious. Only the paranoid survives, but for how long and at what cost? We can turn our eyes to the Savior who could enjoy a deep sleep even through a storm, and in him we too can tune off from the world and close our eyes to slumber as we whisper in prayer, 'Heavenly Father, give us today our daily sleep.'

References

Barber, L., Barnes, C. M., & Carlson, K. (2013). Sleepy respondents: Random and systematic error effects of insomnia on survey behavior. *Organizational Research Methods*, 16, 616–649.

Barnes, C. M. (2011). "I'll sleep when I'm dead": Managing those too busy to sleep. *Organizational Dynamics*, 40, 18–26.

Barnes, C. M., Lucianetti, L., Bhave, D. P., & Christian, M. S. (2015). "You wouldn't like me when I'm sleepy": Leader sleep, daily abusive supervision, and work unit engagement. *Academy of Management Journal*, 58(5), 1419–1437.

Barnes, C. M., Schaubroeck, J. M., Huth, M., & Ghumman, S. (2011). Lack of sleep and unethical behavior. *Organizational Behavior and Human Decision Processes*, 115, 169–180.

Bavinck, H. (1989). Common grace. Trans. Raymond van Leeuwen. *Calvin Theological Journal*, 24(1), 49–61.

Belfort, J. (2007). *The wolf of Wall Street*. Bantam.

Brockner, J., & Higgins, E. T. (2001). Regulatory focus theory: Implications for the study of emotions at work. *Organizational Behavior and Human Decision Processes*, 86, 35–66.

Brueggemann, W. (1993). *Biblical perspectives on evangelism: Living in a three-storied universe*. Nashville, TN: Abingdon.

Champy, J., & Nohria, N. (2000). *The arc of ambition: Defining the leadership journey*. Cambridge, MA: Perseus Publishing.

Giampetro-Meyer, A., Brown, T., Browne, M. N., & Kubasek, N. (1998). Do we really want more leaders in business? *Journal of Business Ethics*, 17(15), 1727–1736.

Iacocca, L. (with William Novak). (1984). *Iacocca, an autobiography*. New York: Bantam Books.

Judge, T. A., & Kammeyer-Mueller, J. D. (2012). On the value of aiming high: The causes and consequences of ambition. *Journal of Applied Psychology*, 97(4), 758.

Lewis, C. S. (1952). *Mere Christianity*. London: Geoffrey Bles.

Lim, J., & Dinges, D. F. (2010). A meta-analysis of the impact of shortterm sleep deprivation on cognitive variables. *Psychological Bulletin*, 136, 375–389.

McClelland, D. C. (1961). *The achieving society*. New York, NY: Van Nostrand.

McClelland, D. C., Atkinson, J. W., Clark, R. A., & Lowell, E. L. (1953). Analysis of imaginative stories for motivational content. In D. C. Mc-Clelland, J. W. Atkinson, R. A. Clark, & E. L. Lowell (Eds.), *The achievement motive* (pp. 107–138). East Norwalk, CT: Appleton-Century-Crofts.

Morris, L. (1984). *1 and 2 Thessalonians* (Tyndale New Testament Commentaries). Nottingham, UK: Intervarsity Press.

Mott, S. C. (1982). *Biblical ethics and social change*. New York: Oxford University Press.

Padilla, A., Hogan, R., & Kaiser, R. B. (2007). The toxic triangle: Destructive leaders, susceptible followers, and conducive environments. *Leadership Quarterly*, 18, 176–194.

Plantinga, C. (1995). *Not the way it's supposed to be: A breviary of sin*. Grand Rapids, MI: W.B. Eerdmans.

Plantinga, C. (2002). *Engaging God's world: A Christian vision of faith, learning, and living*. Grand Rapids, MI: W.B. Eerdmans.

Sendjaya, S., Pekerti, A., Härtel, C., Hirst, G., & Butarbutar, I. (2016). Are authentic leaders always moral? The role of Machiavellianism in the relationship between authentic leadership and morality. *Journal of Business Ethics*, 133(1), 125–139.

Stott, J. R. W. (1984). *Issues facing Christians today*. Basingstoke, England: Marshalls.

Wolterstorff, N. (1983). *Until justice and peace embrace: The Kuyper lectures for 1981 delivered at the Free University of Amsterdam*. Grand Rapids, MI: W.B. Eerdmans.

CHAPTER 7

Don't waste your leadership

*'I'm not afraid of failure. I'm afraid of succeeding
at things that don't matter.'*
William Carey (1761–1834)

Given the presence of indwelling sins, many leaders bear an uncanny resemblance to boiled frogs. Their inability to detect slow, gradual changes make them oblivious to the grave danger they find themselves incapacitated to get out of. Many of us are familiar with the metaphor. Place a frog in a pot of boiling water and it will instinctively jump out, but place it in a pot of lukewarm water and slowly turn up the heat, it will obliviously amuse itself to death.

Why doesn't the frog jump out in a split second? Because its internal apparatus for sensing threat to survival is only designed to detect sudden, dramatic shifts in temperature, not small, incremental changes. It is therefore unable to detect the danger until it's too late to respond (Senge, 1990).

Having spent nearly two decades conducting leadership research and engaging with countless Christian leaders from all walks of life, both within the Christian settings or otherwise (e.g., churches and not-for-profits, government and non-government organizations, small and large corporations), I have observed a slow, gradual shift that occurs as the leader assumes power and enjoys the privileges and perks that come with leadership (e.g., respect, praise, etc.).

This incremental shift manifests in the manner with which they lead people, relative to that exemplified by Christ Jesus himself.

Christian leadership is wasted, albeit slowly and gradually, when Christian leaders' desire does not come *from Christ*, their identity is not secure *in Christ*, their dignity is not aligned *with Christ*, their motive is not oriented *towards Christ*, and their ambition is not set *for* Christ. Let us in turn examine more closely these five areas.

1. When their desire does not flow *from* Christ, they are worshipping idols

Everyone always pursues something in life, and that is naturally human. The desire for attention and recognition, or to be accepted and in control, are hardwired in every individual from birth. When one assumes a leadership position, however, the magnitude of these desires is escalated by virtue of the power and authority he or she possesses.

Think of individuals with meticulous attention to detail and high internal locus of control (i.e., the tendency to attribute success to internal efforts and abilities rather than external influences). If they become leaders, they are prone to the tendency to micro-manage every person within their team or division to ensure compliance with their idiosyncratic standards of excellence in every area. They bark orders, expect perfection, and would remove the under-performers who fall short. I am not saying this is the only plausible pattern, but the intoxicating nature of power often amplify one's deep-seated desires.

Behind the veneer of this overpowering approach to leadership is a craving for control that has gone berserk. In such a scenario, the legitimate desire to be in control has morphed an insatiable neurosis that consumes the leaders' physical and mental attention. It becomes their pursuit of life, the source of comfort (or anxiety), and the object of worship.

For other leaders, that ultimate desire may have nothing do with control. Instead, it could be power, wealth, status, praise, or anything that we deem worth pursuing intensely. Whatever it is, we elevate its status from 'good and legitimate' to 'illegitimate god' (i.e., idol), thereby dethroning the Creator God from his rightful place over our lives. Leaders who are blind to their susceptibility to their own desire will fall victim into idolatry. They find it much easier to play god than to obey God.

The gospel of Jesus Christ helps us to deal with our idolatry of control (or of power, approval, comfort, and so on). Our incessant need to be in control will begin to diminish when we realize that Jesus Christ who is sovereign over all creation voluntarily abandoned control when he left his glory to come to the world and take our place on the cross. We have the courage to jettison our craving for control because we now can put our lives in total surrender to the risen Servant King.

▇ 2. When their identity is not secure *in* Christ, they lead as tyrants or clowns

The second way the enormous privilege of leading is wasted is if leaders base their identity on something else other than Christ, prompting them to lead as self-aggrandizing tyrants or man-pleasing clowns.

Imagine a continuum of leadership approach where tyrants are on one end and clowns on the other. The continuum represents the way we lead. I am not referring to leadership approaches (e.g., servant, authentic, transformational, or some other positive leadership approaches). I am talking about one's overarching perspective in dealing with other people, which gets amplified to the nth degree when the person is entrusted with leadership authority and privileges.

You may know someone who has a disposition to be bossy around people. If that person is put on a position of power and authority, left to his own device, it would be easy for him to turn from being bossy to being self-absorbed tyrants. Similarly, those who always maintain their sense of sanity by securing the approval of others will in leadership roles be more subservient to people's wishes and demands.

Leaders who think and act like tyrants assume that they are the fourth member of the Trinity. Research on destructive leadership have characterized tyrants as malignant narcissists who possess characteristics of grandiosity, defensiveness, deception, intimidation, paranoia, and cruelty. They want to have the final say in every major decision (and even minor ones!), and veto those that they miss.

Unfortunately that is not an atypical phenomenon even within the Christian church. After observing and training Christian leaders in various countries for more than thirty-five years, the late John Stott (2002) wrote the following sober reflection:

> There is too much autocracy in the leaders of the Christian community, in defiance of the teaching of Jesus and His apostles, and not enough love and gentleness. Too many behaved as if they believed not in the priesthood of all believers but in the papacy of all pastors. Our model of leadership is often shaped more by culture than by Christ. Yet many cultural models of leadership are incompatible with the servant imagery taught and exhibited by the Lord Jesus. Nevertheless, these alien cultural models are often transplanted uncritically into the church and its hierarchy.
>
> In Africa it is the tribal chief, in Latin America the exaggerated masculinity of the Spanish male, in South Asia the religious guru fawned on by his disciples, in East Asia the Confucian legacy of the teacher's unchallengeable authority, and in Britain the British Raj mentality.

On the other end of the spectrum, there are clown-like leaders. They are people-pleasers, yes-men or yes-women, who exist to serve others for the sake of securing and maintaining their votes of confidence. These panderers are tolerant and accepting, never demanding anything or holding people accountable. They would dread the thought of having to confront anyone. They would avoid tough decisions that have even the slightest chance to polarize people. They would operate on the basis of expediency, and rely on ingratiation techniques to curry favor from people that matter to them. As such, they lead out of convenience rather than conviction, ensuring that every decision they make will at the end of the day tip the scale in their favor.

When push comes to shove, should a leader be like a tyrant who is feared or a clown who is loved? That is a conundrum that Machiavelli had provided advice for centuries ago (1532, pp. 58–59):

> Upon this a question arises: whether it be better to be loved than feared than loved? It may be answered that one should wish to be both, but, because it is difficult to unite them

in one person, it is much safer to be feared than loved, when, of the two, either must be dispensed with. Because this is to be asserted in general of men, that they are ungrateful, fickle, false, cowardly, covetous . . . and men have less scruple in offending one who is beloved than one who is feared, for love is preserved by the link of obligation which, owing to the baseness of men, is broken at every opportunity for their advantage; but fear preserves you by a dread of punishment which never fails.

Countless corporate executives today religiously follow the Machiavellian advice to lead by fear rather than by love. In fact, Machiavelli's book *The Prince* is used as a corporate manual for employee orientation in companies like Enron (now defunct).

In contrast, Jesus taught and exemplified a radically different approach during his ministry on earth. He was unlike a tyrant who seeks to be feared but not loved. Yet he was also unlike a clown whose preoccupation is to be loved but not feared. Because Jesus was full of grace and truth (John 1:14), he led with grace and truth. That does not mean 50% grace and 50% truth at any given time. Or 100% grace half of the time, and 100% truth the other half. Rather all grace, all truth, all the time.

He led and acted with such authority that people around him made a verbal remark about it, yet showed mercy and compassion towards those who are marginalized by the system. He was often very forthright to his disciples, calling them out, warning and rebuking them, yet extended incredible patience towards them when they were too slow to learn, or simply clueless. He spoke the truth in love.

Being simultaneously graceful and truthful is key to guard leaders from shapeshifting into tyrants or clowns. Truthful leadership without grace will result in tyranny, and graceful leadership without truth will result in anarchy.

3. When their dignity is not aligned *with* Christ, they adopt the way of the world and abort the way of the cross

While it is clearly that the bible is not a leadership book, it contains the most profound principles, patterns, and practices of leadership that have been either neglected or misunderstood by many leaders.

That is the reason why even Christian leaders tend to abort them and instead adopt principles, patterns, and practices of the world.

But here is the irony of ironies. I have been observing for many years now a tragic megatrend that is occurring everywhere across the four corners of the globe. Businesses, often perceived as secular and slippery, have increasingly adopted biblical leadership principles (albeit in their own secular ways), while on the other hand churches have aborted them.

By churches, I do not refer to buildings, denominations, or institutions. Nor do I refer to God's people who are congregating every Sunday for worship. I do not refer to the church gathered, but the church dispersed, namely God's people who work every day in various walks of life (e.g., janitors, kindergarten teachers, company executives, heads of states).

The abortion and adoption process can be observed in many areas. Take vision, for example. Vision is no doubt a biblical concept. The oldest document that explicitly and teaches vision is the Bible. 'Where there is no prophetic vision the people cast off restraint' (Proverbs 29:18). If you are a biblical scholar, you would quickly point out to me that this particular verse does *not* refer to the importance of leadership vision in organizations (or the church for that matter), as many Christian leadership authors have claimed. And you are absolutely right! Reading that interpretation into the text would be an exegetical fallacy (Carson, 1996).

Rather vision in the bible signifies God's revelation to his people so that they live in accordance to and not wander away from his laws. That God reveals the direction he wants his people to follow is a theme that is continuously repeated in both the Old and New Testaments, from Abraham to apostle Paul.

However, extrapolated to a larger context, the verse has obvious practical implications for Christian leaders. First, as God's appointed leaders, they should take their people to the direction that is set only by God. Just like the Israelites of old who relied on the pillar of cloud and pillar of fire from God, they need to know when to go and when to stop. It is right for them to take a risk in the omniscient God who never takes risk. It is wrong for them to trek outside the perceptive will of God. Without clarity of such vision, what they do will eventually be a case of the blind leading the blind.

Second, Christian leaders need to operate within boundaries set by God. Obedience is needed for matters that are explicitly prescribed in the written revelation of God, and wisdom for matters that are only implicitly mentioned. For example, a Christian leader should always decline the offer to compromise their individual and corporate integrity for the sake of expediency, no matter how appealing the offer might seem at the outset. However, the same leader might need a biblical discernment to be able to make the tough, unpopular decision to, for example, retrench a high-performing senior manager who proves to be a serial bully at work. That means doing it with truth and grace and in a civilized and humane manner.

In short, the biblical concept of vision is still relevant for contemporary leadership today (as are other biblical concepts such as accountability, empowerment, authenticity, etc.). Unfortunately, it has been detached today from Christian leadership in many quarters. If a poll is taken from a random sample of people on the street, asking them which institution in the world comes to mind when they hear the word *vision*, I would bet the answer will not be the church of Jesus Christ. Invariably they would mention global companies such as Coca-Cola or Disney. These companies can penetrate individuals across the globe with a very strong brand image because they fully understand the importance of the vision and pursue it relentlessly for decades.

Granted the way they understand vision is different from the biblical understanding mentioned above. That is, God's revealed will is nowhere to be found in their vision statement or strategic documents. My point however is they have a simple and clear mental image of the future that has captured the imaginations of people from all walks of life.

The vision of Coca-Cola was set in the 1930s by its president Robert Woodruff: 'We will see every person gets a bottle of Coke for five cents, wherever they are and whatever it costs.' After more than eight decades, we see that that same direction is still vigorously pursued, and today we witness that the world is moving closer to the reality. Disney, another household name, was founded by Walter Elias Disney, who had a dream of establishing 'the happiest place on earth'.

Dozens of other companies can be cited to illustrate how non-Christian leaders seem to adopt the concept of vision originated in the bible whereas Christian leaders seem to abort it. Business journalists will continue to report on how the most valued and respected global companies in the world continue to achieve their vision, oblivious to the fact that they are hijacking the concept from the bible. Peter Drucker (1989), the father of modern management, wrote a landmark article three decades ago entitled *What Business Can Learn from Nonprofits*. What is now needed is perhaps the opposite: *What Churches Can Learn from Businesses*.

4. When their motive is not oriented *towards* Christ, the people they lead are growing into their likeness

The fourth area where Christian leadership has been wasted has to do with the question, 'What are the leaders turning the followers into?' Leadership is not about creating the 'mini-me' version of the leaders. Countless followers of charismatic leaders think, talk, even walk like their idolized leaders. Projecting their needs into their leaders-turned-messiah is undoubtedly foolish because no leader can fulfil what only Christ can.

I am not saying that Christian leaders cannot be role models. They should be. Yet they are not the ultimate prototype that every follower ought to emulate. Christian leaders are worth following to the extent they follow Christ.

Ask yourself, 'To what extent can I say like the apostle Paul, "Follow me, as I follow Christ"?' Can you say that for every single area of your life, e.g., work, family, finance, personal growth, life priority, time management, pastime?

An important caveat is warranted here. Because no one is infallible, no individual leader can reflect Christ in every single area. It is therefore dangerous for us to follow only one leader. What we need in every institution is a plurality of leaders to ensure accountable and sustainable leadership of the organization. This is true for business, government, public, or not-for-profit organizations, even churches.

Within the church context, having multiple leaders is not so much the issue of denominational governance structure (e.g., Presbyterian, Reformed, Baptist, Episcopalian) as it is spiritual

wisdom. The issue is not about applying the right church governance structure because what often happens in many churches is
that the senior pastor or lay leader with the strongest personality
rules like a sovereign king, regardless of their governance structure. An authoritarian, control-freak leader in a Reformed church
governance structure can be very domineering or overpowering,
blatantly ignoring the Reformed principle of church eldership.

This phenomenon is all too common particularly in highly paternalistic cultures where the top leaders assume they are wise and
godly in every sphere of life twenty-four hours a day, seven days
a week. They act as if the whole counsel of God resides in them
and them alone. They refuse to submit to the authority of God
manifested through the body of leaders.

In fact, leadership studies unequivocally show that the 'great
man' leadership approach has caused severe adverse effects on
individuals and organizations of all sorts. If there is anything that
history has repeatedly taught us on the danger of solo leadership,
it is the untold misery and damages caused by charismatic, larger-
than-life individuals (typically male) while they are in the process
of building a business empire, transforming an industry, leading a
social revolution, or founding a new denomination.

Of course, what they do might spur growth in the key performance indicators, whatever those indicators are. But individuals
are being deceived, manipulated, and bullied. They learn to be
dependent on the leader, and in turn are never able to stand on their
own two feet. As with all grossly unbiblical errors, these pseudo-
leaders will be held accountable either in this side of heaven or in
front of the bema of Christ.

5. When their ambition is not set *for* Christ, they build their own kingdom

There are various mechanisms of leadership selection and
succession, a vast subject of scholarly studies in the field of
organizational leadership. Irrespective of whether leaders are
elected by the public, representatives of that public, institutional
members, or by popular votes, they become leaders because of
some collective decisions made by man and later confirmed by
the leaders.

Leadership selection decision is invariably made on the basis of the candidate's level of experience, achievements, capacities, charisma, or a combination of all those factors. Often these factors were prioritized over and above, or even to the exclusion of the notion of calling.

The key question for the leadership selection committee is, 'Does God call that person to be a leader'? That is a very abstract question, but can be operationalized to the following more practical question. 'To what extent are indicators of a godly character exemplified in 1 Timothy 3 or Titus 1 (for example) exhibited by the candidate, irrespective of his or her, say, charisma?'

It will be remiss for the committee to base their decisions predominantly on the candidate's charisma in public speaking. Research shows that while charisma might bolster leaders to exert their personal influence, it is not a necessary quality for effective leadership. In fact, scholars agree that charisma might pose more lethal danger than benefits, both for the leaders and the organization they lead (Howell & Avolio, 1992).

For the individual candidate, the focal question is, 'Does God want me to take up that leadership role?' The need to carefully discern whether it is the individuals' natural ambition or God's divine appointment is paramount to Christian leadership. The degree to which the process involves a prayerful and thoughtful deliberation of God's call over and above one's ambition for power, prestige, or popularity will determine the effectiveness of that individual leader, particularly in the long run.

As discussed previously, the issue here is not that personal ambition is necessarily bad. We should not pit human ambition against divine calling. Ambition or, more precisely, a sanctified ambition is actually a prerequisite for effective Christian leadership. However, a raw and sinful ambition for prestige, power, or popularity creates a danger not only for the individual leader, but also to others within the proximal and distal reach of the leader.

A final note for those unwilling to lead and unwilling to quit

As we reach the end of the book, I would like to address two groups of readers in particular: Those who are unwilling to lead and those who are unwilling to quit. If after reading thus far you think you might have the capacity to lead but not the willingness, please read this section carefully. If you think you feel both the urge and fear to step down, please read it slowly.

Leaders who are hesitant to lead and leaders who refuse to step down essentially have the same issue. They are both crippled by fear and pride. The former fear that they would fail and are too proud to admit it. The latter fear they would be irrelevant and are anxious about the prospect of losing the status and respect they have immensely enjoyed as leaders. Both are being played by the idols of their heart.

Where do these fear and pride originate? They are implanted in hearts by a coalition force comprising the devil, the world, and their own flesh. In other words, it is an inside job. As such, the solution cannot possibly lie within the reluctant or ambitious leaders.

You might resort to the secular approaches. The oft-cited recommendation to boost self-efficacy (i.e., 'you can if you think you can!'), for example, will only make your sense of pride swollen to the nth degree. Even evidence-based solutions in the final analysis would merely be touch-up jobs that do not bring deep and lasting transformation. The only solution that works is the Gospel of Christ, which demolishes both fear and pride simultaneously.

Here is how the Gospel relates to leaders' fear. If Jesus Christ was willing to die for me when I was still actively opposing him (i.e., the greatest mistake a person can do to his/her Redeemer), I can have the confidence that he would never reject me.

If Christ, the ultimate being in whom, by whom, and through whom all things visible and invisible have been created, will never ever reject me, I should never fear rejection from anyone on this planet for they are far less significant in stature than Christ. As such, I can take up a leadership role with *confidence*, and I can step down from that leadership role with *contentment*.

Here is how the Gospel relates to leaders' pride. If Jesus Christ did not merely send a warning sign but had to come to the fallen world to save me from myself, I must be a totally wretched person. Regardless of my performance and achievements, I was essentially a hell-bent serial sinner that deserved God's full wrath.

Since Christ took my place on that rugged cross, I should no longer worry about losing face if I fail. Instead I would say, 'I am a weak sinner, I cannot do this leadership role alone, but I can do it through Christ who strengthens me.' I also should not be anxious about stepping down. Instead I would say, 'I am a dispensable sinner. I'm only a created, limited, and polluted human being with an expiry date. The show will go on without me.'

It took me a long while to let this gospel truth simmer in my heart. I cannot emphasize its importance for my own personal leadership journey. Preach it to your soul. Meditate on it. Apply it. Discuss it with others. Teach it to your staff.

For the sake of Christ and his people, those of you who are reluctant to lead, lead! And those who are reluctant to quit, quit!

References

Carson, D. A. (1996). *Exegetical fallacies* (2nd ed.). Ada, MI: Baker Academic.

Drucker, P. (1989). What business can learn from nonprofits. *Harvard Business Review*, 67(4), 88–93.

Howell, J. M., & Avolio, B. J. (1992). The ethics of charismatic leadership: Submission or liberation? *Academy of Management Perspective*, 6(2), 42–54.

Machiavelli, N. (1532). *The Prince* (Q. Skinner & R. Price, Trans., 16th ed., 2004). Cambridge: Cambridge University Press.

Senge, P. M. (1990). *The fifth discipline: The art and practice of the learning organization*. New York: Doubleday/Currency.

Stott, J. (2002). *Calling Christian leaders: Biblical models of church, gospel and ministry* (p. 130). InterVarsity Press.

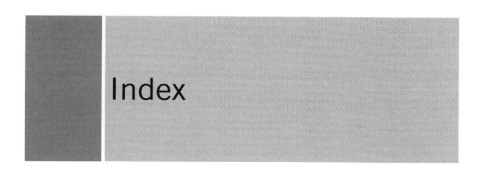

Index